PSYCHOLOGY PRACTITIONER GUIDEBOOKS

EDITORS

Arnold P. Goldstein, Syracuse University
Leonard Krasner, Stanford University & SUNY at Stony Brook
Sol L. Garfield, Washington University in St. Louis

BEHAVIORAL RELAXATION TRAINING AND ASSESSMENT

ROGER POPPEN

Southern Illinois University at Carbondale

PERGAMON PRESS

New York · Oxford · Beijing · Frankfurt
São Paulo · Sydney · Tokyo · Toronto

U.S.A.	Pergamon Press, Inc., Maxwell House, Fairview Park, Elmsford, New York 10523, U.S.A.
U.K.	Pergamon Press plc, Headington Hill Hall, Oxford OX3 0BW, England
PEOPLE'S REPUBLIC OF CHINA	Pergamon Press, Room 4037, Qianmen Hotel, Beijing, People's Republic of China
FEDERAL REPUBLIC OF GERMANY	Pergamon Press GmbH, Hammerweg 6, D-6242 Kronberg, Federal Republic of Germany
BRAZIL	Pergamon Editora Ltda, Rua Eça de Queiros, 346, CEP 04011, Paraiso, São Paulo, Brazil
AUSTRALIA	Pergamon Press Australia Pty Ltd., P.O. Box 544, Potts Point, N.S.W. 2011, Australia
JAPAN	Pergamon Press, 5th Floor, Matsuoka Central Building, 1-7-1 Nishishinjuku, Shinjuku-ku, Tokyo 160, Japan
CANADA	Pergamon Press Canada Ltd., Suite No. 271, 253 College Street, Toronto, Ontario, Canada M5T 1R5

Copyright © 1988 Pergamon Books, Inc.

First edition 1988

Library of Congress Cataloging in Publication Data

Poppen, Roger.
Behavioral relaxation training and assessment/Roger Poppen.
p.   cm. — (Psychology practitioner guidebooks)
Bibliography: p.
Includes indexes.
1. Relaxation — Study and teaching — Philosophy.
2. Relaxation — Methodology.   3. Behaviorism
(Psychology)   I. Title.   II. Series.
BF637.R45P66   1988   158'.9 — oc19   88-463

British Library Cataloguing in Publication Data

Poppen, Roger
  Behavioral relaxation training and assessment.
  1. Medicine.   Relaxation therapy
  I. Title.   II. Series
  615.8'51

ISBN 0-08-035566-8 Hardcover
ISBN 0-08-035565-X Flexicover

Printed in Great Britain by A. Wheaton & Co., Ltd., Exeter

To my students,
who have taught me much

Contents

Preface   ix

Acknowledgement   x

Chapter

1. A Behavioral Analysis of Relaxation   1

2. Assessment of Relaxation   19

3. Behavioral Relaxation Training   50

4. BRT with Special Populations   70

5. Applications and Extrapolations   92

Appendix A: BRS Score Sheet   123

Appendix B: Written Criterion Tests for BRS Observers   124

Appendix C: Self-Report Scale   126

Appendix D: Home Practice Form   127

References   128

Author Index   133

Subject Index   135

About the Author   137

Series List   138

Preface

This book presents a behavior analytic approach to relaxation training and application. Behavior analysis is a useful system for organizing current knowledge of complex human behavior, and for guiding research into the many areas yet unknown. For those readers unfamiliar with this point of view, or who believe it to be limited in application to the simple behavior of simple organisms, I would like to set down briefly the major assumptions of this approach. These are gleaned from the writings of B. F. Skinner, who for the past fifty years has pointed the way to a comprehensive science and technology of human behavior (Skinner, 1953, 1957, 1969, 1974, 1987).

A BEHAVIORIST'S CATECHISM

First, *behavior is the dependent variable*. The behavior of an individual is the event to be accounted for and, in educational and therapeutic contexts, changed.

Second, *the social and physical environment is the independent variable*. Educational, therapeutic, and research settings are constructed in order to assess and alter the behavior of the student/client/subject. Neurophysiologic, biochemical, genetic, and similar organismic structural variables have important influences on behavior, but are not prerequisites for understanding and changing behavior. In fact, the effects of structural variables can only be determined when environmental variables are adequately known.

Third, *behavior and environment interact in a dynamic relationship*, termed a *contingency*. *Antecedents* refer to the environmental setting or occasion in which the behavior of interest occurs. *Consequences* refer to the changes in the environment wrought by the behavior. *History* refers to prior contingencies that influence current behavior. *Learning* refers to changes in behavior wrought by the contingencies.

Fourth, behavior is often *complex*, comprised of several interacting elements. (Later, I present a four-component system of behavior and propose that an exclusive focus on any single component may be misleading.) Complexity arises from behavior in many modalities occurring simultaneously, and from 'chains' of behavior extending over time, in which earlier 'links' influence later ones. Such *inter-behavioral control* does not violate principles one, two and three.

Fifth, *covert* behavior adds an extra dimension of complexity. Behavior 'beneath the skin', which is observable only to the individual so engaged, may influence publicly observable behavior and vice versa. Private behavior is ultimately influenced by environmental contingencies operating upon its public connections.

Sixth, *verbal behavior* is especially important. Humans are social creatures and verbal behavior is our primary medium of social interaction. *Rules* are verbal statements of contingencies which can reveal, conceal, enhance, or compete with physical and social contingencies in the control of behavior.

Seventh, *self-control* is achieved by applying the same variables by which we influence others' behavior to ourselves. It occurs within a larger context of social contingencies.

Behavior analysis has made its mark in the improvement of life for persons with limited verbal skills or those living in highly controlled environments. However, this is just a beginning phase. As more is learned about items five, six, and seven, behavior analysis will continue to make contributions to the lives of more verbal and autonomous people.

Relaxation is a complex behavior that plays an important role in many therapeutic programs. Current views of relaxation have grown out of physiologic, personality, and cognitive psychology. This book presents a behavior analysis point of view. It has two purposes. One is to provide a general framework to organize and guide research and application of relaxation training procedures. The other is to present new training and assessment procedures based on the behavioral tradition.

ACKNOWLEDGEMENTS

Appreciation is expressed to LiMing R. Poppen for the illustrations of relaxed postures, with thanks also to Maria Watson-Perczel for posing. The contributions of the following people for their assistance on various projects is gratefully acknowledged: Laura Davis, Paul Erlandson, Edward Jiang, Fred Ribet, David Rush, David Sievert, and David Wheeler.

Chapter One

A Behavioral Analysis of Relaxation

Relaxation training, in its many guises, is a major component in the behavioral treatment of most anxiety, stress, and pain disorders. Hundreds of published articles, ranging from clinical case reports to multi-factorial controlled group designs, attest to the effectiveness of relaxation training, or treatment 'packages' containing relaxation, in the treatment of these disorders. Yet for all its popularity in application, the phenomenon of relaxation itself has received relatively little attention. Training is often employed in a 'cookbook' fashion, with only vague or speculative notions about how or why it may be effective. Researchers and practitioners seldom measure what their trainees are doing and how it is related to treatment outcome (Luiselli, Marholin, Steinman & Steinman, 1979). Training procedures proliferate, with this book presenting yet another one. But without a rational and empirical basis, the trainer has little guidance in selecting from the various techniques and in evaluating his or her choice. One purpose of this book is to provide such guidance.

This first chapter presents an overview of current theories of relaxation and methods of training. It maintains a behavioral orientation, emphasizing the physical and social environment of the training and the behavior of the trainee. The goal is to provide a common framework by which to organize the diversity of procedures and behaviors that control the professional use of the term 'relaxation.' This chapter also provides the foundation for the behavioral assessment and training procedures described in subsequent chapters.

THEORIES OF RELAXATION

Most theories of relaxation appeal to physiologic mechanisms. Some have empirical foundations, while others merely speculate about physiologic processes. It is beyond the scope of this book to critically review the physiologic literature, but the utility of theories based on the 'conceptual nervous system' must be questioned. Some theories propose that relaxation is a single state or condition, while others propose that there are two or more types or components of relaxation. These are discussed as *unitary, dualistic,* and *multimodal* theories.

Unitary Theories

Pride of place goes to Edmund Jacobson (1929; 1934; 1938) who can be called the father of relaxation. He developed *progressive relaxation,* which is the basis of the most common training procedures employed in the United States. He also developed electromyographic (EMG) methods of assessment. He championed the use of relaxation for a diverse range of maladies, providing case reports of its effectiveness.

Muscular Theory. Jacobson defined relaxation as the quiescence of skeletel muscle activity, as measured peripherally by the EMG. At the neurologic level, he proposed a diminished motoneuron output and a reduced proprioceptive input, citing as evidence his research on the reduced magnitude and increased latency of spinal reflexes when a person is relaxed. He further proposed that, as a result of reduced afferent and efferent activity in the skeletel motor system, autonomic and cortical arousal is decreased, citing anatomic and physiologic data supporting a correlation between these systems. Thus neuromuscular relaxation could have salutory effects on diverse physiologic, 'neurotic', and 'emotional' disorders which involve cortical and autonomic structures. Later research on animals has verified that posterior hypothalamic and sympathetic arousal are directly related to muscular proprioceptive activity (Gellhorn & Loofbourrow, 1963).

Autonomic Theory. Later writers have chosen to emphasize the autonomic rather than the muscular aspects of relaxation. The involvement of autonomically innervated visceral structures in emotional and stress disorders, as well as the reciprocal relationship between the sympathetic and parasympathetic branches of the autonomic nervous system, have provided an easily understood 'mechanism' of relaxation and its action. Joseph Wolpe (1958), a major founder of the discipline of behavior therapy, revived the dormant procedure of Jacobson. His adaptation of progressive relaxation training was a central feature of systematic desensitization, a clinical procedure which opened the door to behavioral treatments of anxiety disorders. Wolpe conceived of relaxation as the parasympathetic antithesis of sympathetically-mediated anxiety. According to this view, the parasympathetic state of relaxation 'reciprocally inhibited' the sympathetic state of anxiety.

Herbert Benson, an important figure in the discipline known as behavioral medicine, and his colleagues, also presented a parasympathetic theory of relaxation, emphasizing its effects on various medical conditions (Benson, 1975; Benson, Beary, & Carol, 1974; Wallace, Benson, & Wilson, 1971). Although Benson employed meditation rather than progressive relaxation, the common denominator of all techniques was held to be parasympathetic activity.

According to this view, relaxation represents a shift in autonomic activity away from sympathetic dominance toward parasympathetic dominance. A relaxed state thus is characterized by any of a number of parasympathetically-mediated visceral activities, such as decreased heart rate, respiratory rate, blood pressure, and oxygen consumption. One would also expect relaxation to inhibit visceral activities mediated solely by the sympathetic system, resulting in increased peripheral vasodilation and skin resistance.

Three problems exist with the parasympathetic theory, one conceptual, one empirical, and one practical.

Conceptually, it is not clear which visceral systems should show parasympathetic dominance during relaxation. A widely held view is that relaxation is a trophotropic, or energy-restorative, response, providing homeostatic balance for the ergotropic 'fight-or-flight' response (Benson *et al.*, 1974; Gellhorn & Loofbourrow, 1963; Hess, 1957; Stoyva, 1976). One might think a unitary trophotropic system would include digestive secretions, gastric motility, and sexual tumescence. Though restorative in function, these parasympathetic actions are not usually considered to be components of relaxation. A related problem is that parasympathetic activity is not universally benign: vasodilation in migraine, bronchial constriction in asthma, and acid secretion in gastric ulcer are but a few examples of destructive parasympathetic activity. According to this theory, such conditions should be exacerbated by relaxation. But instead, relaxation methods are often used as part of treatment programs for these disorders.

One might seek to avoid this conceptual problem by empirically defining relaxation as those parasympathetic activities which change as a result of relaxation training. However, despite decades of research, there is no set of parasympathetic responses which is consistently related to all relaxation training procedures for all trainees, or even to a particular procedure for persons in a particular diagnostic category (Hillenberg & Collins, 1982; Holmes, 1984; Qualls & Sheehan, 1981). Failure to find an expected change in a particular autonomic system may be due to an inappropriate definition of relaxation, an inadequate training procedure, or an idiosyncratic trainee. This is not to deny that relaxation procedures result in autonomic changes, and that these changes may be beneficial to some individuals. The empirical problem is just that we do not yet know which training variables in combination with which individual variables result in what autonomic outcomes. A blanket 'parasympathetic' theory provides no guidance in answering these questions.

Finally, a practical problem with this theory is that autonomic measures are cumbersome, expensive, intrusive, and reactive to a variety of variables unrelated to relaxation. Because of these problems, physiologic assessment of relaxation is generally ignored, except in special research settings. Consequently, an autonomic conceptualization of relaxation offers the clinician no way to determine how well the trainee is learning the skill of relaxation.

Summary. Among the unitary theories, Jacobson advocated a muscular basis for relaxation, while Wolpe, Benson, and other noted investigators have emphasized parasympathetic activity. Although a *de facto* consensus exists in terms of frequently employed measures of relaxation (e.g., frontalis EMG, heart rate, blood pressure, electrodermal activity, skin temperature, and oxygen uptake), no consistent evidence for the necessity or sufficiency of these measures exists. In addition, as will be shown in subsequent sections, many investigators believe that relaxation involves more than a pattern of physiologic activity, whatever those patterns may prove to be.

On the training side of the equation, Jacobson and Wolpe employed muscular tense–release exercises, while Benson employed a secular form of meditation. Benson went further to propose a unitary training theory, in that all relaxation training procedures are comprised of the same basic ingredients. This notion will be discussed in later portions of this chapter.

Dualistic Theories

The contemporary version of the ancient separation of human behavior into 'mind' and 'body' is the distinction between 'cognitive' and 'somatic'. Some investigators have applied these concepts to relaxation, suggesting that they describe distinct aspects of relaxation and of the various training methods (Davidson & Schwartz, 1976; Heide & Borkovec, 1983; Lehrer, Woolfolk, Rooney, McCann & Carrington, 1983). As an aside, it should be noted that the proponents of this view discuss relaxation in the context of its antithesis, anxiety, which is also seen as having both cognitive and somatic components.

Cognitive and Somatic Relaxation. According to this view, somatic relaxation consists of the muscular, visceral, or neurologic processes described by unitary theories. In addition to, or sometimes in place of, direct measures of somatic activity, investigators employ self-report ratings on the occurrence of various physical symptoms (e.g., the Cognitive–Somatic Anxiety Questionnaire, in Schwartz, Davidson, & Goleman, 1978). Like the unitary theorists, dualists do not provide clarification as to which of the somatic activities are necessary or sufficient for relaxation. Nor have they demonstrated a clear-cut relationship between self-report ratings and actual physiologic measures.

Cognitive relaxation consists of a subjective experience of calmness. It is usually measured in negative terms, as low ratings of anxiety, worry, or other undesirable mental states, on various self-report scales. Although Davidson and Schwartz (1976) discuss the use of electrodermal and electroencephalographic measures of cognitive activity, the ultimate criterion for subjective experience has to be the individual's report of it. As such, it is taken at face value, and validation is considered only in terms of intercorrelations among various self-report scales.

Relaxation training procedures are also separated into cognitive and somatic categories, depending on whether the behaviors of the trainee are predominantly in one or the other realm. Of the methods described previously, progressive relaxation is categorized as a somatic method while meditation is catagorized as a cognitive method (Cauthen & Prymak, 1977; Lehrer *et al.*, 1983; Schwartz *et al.*, 1978).

Research has taken the form of comparing groups of persons trained in progressive relaxation with groups trained in meditation on a large number and variety of physiologic and self-report measures. One goal of such research has been to show that cognitive training affects cognitive measures and somatic training affects somatic measures. Another goal has been to show that people who differ on various measures of cognitive and somatic anxiety will respond differently to the two training procedures. The most general finding is that both progressive relaxation and meditation training produce changes in a therapeutic direction on both self-report and physiological measures, which is interpreted as supporting a 'generalized relaxation response' (Lehrer *et al.*, 1983; Schwartz *et al.*, 1978). However, these effects may be no greater than those resulting from placebo or rest procedures (Benson & Friedman, 1985; Holmes, 1984; Peveler & Johnston, 1986). With respect to differences between cognitive and somatic procedures and measures, statistically significant differences between groups have been found on a few measures, but given the large number of dependent variables employed, confirmation of the reliability of such differences awaits replication.

Other investigators have examined the adverse reactions that people sometimes exhibit in relaxation training, suggesting that some people with cognitive anxiety may react negatively to somatic training, while those with somatic anxiety may react negatively to cognitive training (Heide & Borkovec, 1983). Further examination of 'relaxation-induced anxiety' has suggested that some people respond anxiously to the various 'somatic' and 'cognitive' events that occur during training, depending on their pre-existing sensitivities; however, the relationships between particular predispositions and particular events are by no means clear, either theoretically or empirically (Heide & Borkovec, 1984).

Summary. Dualistic theories propose that just as anxiety may be more or less mental or physical, relaxation behavior and the various training methods are similarly divided. The goal of this approach is to provide a rationale for the observation that not all training procedures work equally well for all individuals. The categorization of disorders and training procedures along cognitive and somatic dimensions provides a basis for selecting among the various methods and predicting the most efficacious outcome. Davidson and Schwartz (1976) propose that somatic relaxation methods have greater effects on somatic anxiety, while cognitive methods are better for cognitive anxiety. In a similar vein, Heide and Borkovec (1983) suggest that the phenomenon of 'relaxation-induced anxiety' may be related to the unfortunate combination of a category of training method with a type of pre-training anxiety condition.

Unfortunately, many difficulties lie in the definition and measurement of subjective states. Self-report inventories of somatic and cognitive behavior have multiplied, offering a bewildering variety of measures. As with unitary approaches, there is also a large variety of physiologic measures from which to choose. Occasional statistical relations among this multitude of measures do not lead to confidence that 'cognitive' and 'somatic' behaviors are reliably measured or are consistently related to training variables.

Multimodal Theories

Multimodal theories propose that there are three or more categories of relaxation. Some can be viewed as expansions of the dualistic model, adding new dimensions or unfolding existing ones. In contrast, the approach of this book rejects the separation of 'mind' and 'body', proposing that relaxation is a response class across four behavior modalities.

A Twelve-Category Theory. Davidson and Schwartz (1976) embellished their basic dualistic theory, adding a third mode of behavior, termed 'attentional', which refers to the 'restriction' and 'opening up' of 'awareness'. Cutting across these three broad categories, they also proposed a dimension of cortical hemispheric specialization ('right-brain' and 'left-brain' activation), as well as an 'active–passive' dimension. This three (cognitive/somatic/attentional) by two (right-brain/left-brain) by two (active/passive) system leads to twelve possible categories of relaxation. Additional dimensions, such as internally generated or externally occurring stimuli, further complicate the picture.

The primary purpose of a categorization scheme is to clarify, and in this respect the Davidson and Schwartz system is not successful. First, it is not clear how 'attention' and 'awareness' processes are separate from the 'cognitive' mode of behavior. *Cognition* would seem to be a general term, encompassing a number of mental processes, with *attention* being a subset of these processes. This points up the difficulty in defining 'cognitive' states. Second, 'hemispheric specialization' appears to be a neurologic metaphor for certain types of behavior. The activity of the brain is not directly observed but inferred from behavior. Greater clarity could be achieved by describing the behavior and the conditions under which it occurs, rather than the hypothetical activity of neural structures or psychological states. Finally, the 'activity' dimension is included to account for the fact that in some instances physical activity, such as jogging or dance, may be relaxing. But it is not clear if these are to be regarded as relaxation techniques, or simply that one can feel relaxed (or not) while engaging in any number of activities, from walking to sky-diving.

A positive contribution of the Davidson and Schwartz theory is the idea that relaxation consists of many classes of behavior, and that various training methods emphasize different aspects of relaxation. Also inherent in this system is the idea that various disorders involve maladaptive activity in a particular response mode, and that a relaxation procedure which emphasizes that mode will be most therapeutic. While Davidson and Schwartz were primarily concerned with anxiety, this notion can be expanded to include other maladies.

A Tripartite Theory. Schilling and Poppen (1983) applied Lang's (1968) conceptualization of anxiety measurement to relaxation. Lang proposed an operational definition of fear, involving three types of measurement corresponding to three response systems: behavioral, verbal, and physiological. In a fearsome situation, one can observe the person's overt behavior, namely avoidance; his or her self-report (a fear rating); and his or her physiological activity (any one of numerous autonomic and EMG measures). In essence, this system modifies the dualistic approach, restricting 'cognition' to verbal behavior and splitting the 'somatic' component into parts observed with and without electronic equipment. Schilling and Poppen noted that relaxation could be similarly observed and measured in terms of the trainee's overt postures, verbal report, and physiological activity.

This approach also has certain limitations. First, operational definitions emphasize the behavior of the observer more than the trainee. The three categories refer to whether the observer is watching the trainee, listening to (or reading) the trainee's self-reports, or employing electronic instruments. The same action of the trainee could be classed as 'behavioral' or 'physiologic' depending on whether the observer watched the person or an EMG device. Second, this approach ignores certain topographic aspects of the person's actions. Thus, a person may 'avoid' a situation by running way, jabbering incessantly, or covering his or her eyes and ears. Third, it also ignores certain functional aspects of a response. For example, a self-report might be controlled by an internal feeling, a request by the investigator, or a desire to change the topic. Fourth, limiting the use of the term 'behavior' to overt actions implies that verbal and physiological activities are something other than behaviors. All directly observable activity is 'behavior,' and more descriptive terms should be found. Along these lines, identifying 'cognitive' behavior as only 'verbal' seems to omit many other behaviors to which 'cognition', however vaguely, seems to refer.

On the positive side, this approach does suggest that various 'states', such as emotions and relaxation, can be thought of as complex behaviors, made up of co-varying components. The particular state depends upon the particular mix of components. Also, as suggested by Schilling and Poppen, various relaxation training procedures can be seen as emphasizing particular modes of behavior. This theory served as one of the antecedents for the following approach, which sought to address the limitations listed above.

Four Modality Theory: A Behavioral Taxonomy. Poppen (in press) has presented a behavioral taxonomy for the analysis of complex behavior which can be applied to relaxation. This system adheres to the level of observable behavior and does not propose explanations in mental, chemical, or neurological realms. According to this theory, complex behavior, such as relaxation, involves responding in four behavioral domains. Various approaches to relaxation emphasize one or another of these modes and ignore or downplay others. This behavioral taxonomy delineates all the domains of behavior in which relaxation can occur, providing a framework for the analysis of interactions between the various aspects of relaxation behavior, as well as for the analysis of various training methods.

As shown in Table 1.1, there are four general categories of behavior, termed *motoric, verbal, visceral,* and *observational*. Behavior may be categorized according to both its functional and structural properties.

Table 1.1. A Taxonomy of Behavior with Examples of Relaxation

Behavior modality	Function	Relaxation Examples
Motoric	Manipulates physical environment.	Overt: Relaxed postures. Covert: Low muscle tension.
Verbal	Manipulates social environment.	Overt: Rating scale. Covert: Silent mantra.
Visceral	Maintains internal environment.	Overt: Slow respiration. Covert: Low heart rate.
Observational	Seeks and differentiates stimuli.	Overt: Closed eyes. Covert: 'Calm' imagery.

While recognizing that neurophysiologic and biochemical structures underlie behavior, this approach emphasizes its functional properties.

Each of these modes of behavior is further divided into two aspects: overt behavior, which is publicly observable, and covert behavior, observable only to the individual so engaged. A key requirement is that behavior is directly observable without the use of intrusive instruments. *Overt behavior* can be observed by others—seen, heard, or palpated. *Covert behavior* can be observed—felt or sensed as well as 'seen' or 'heard'—by an audience of one, the behaving person. Below is a description of each of the four behavior modalities and relaxed behaviors that may occur in each.

Motoric behavior, as the name implies, functions to move the body and to manipulate the physical environment. Structurally, it involves the skeletal/muscular system. Motoric behavior is controlled by the contingencies of physical and social reinforcement, including imitative and instructional control.

Relaxed motoric behavior is characterized by low levels of muscle tension in muscle groups not required for posture or movement. Low levels of tension are characterized by overt relaxed postures, which will be described more completely in chapters 2 and 3. Covert muscle tension may be observed and reported by the trainee, requiring observational and verbal behavior. Jacobson invented electromyography (EMG) to provide an overt measure of covert muscle tension, though as Skinner (1969) noted, 'the scales read by the scientist are not the same as the private events themselves.' In settings where action is required, relaxed motoric behavior is smooth and rhythmic. Unrelaxed motoric behavior involves unnecessary tension and jerky, abrupt movements.

Verbal behavior functions to mediate social reinforcement (Skinner, 1957). It is the primary means of manipulating, and being manipulated by, one's social environment. Structurally, the human vocal system is dedicated to verbal behavior, though motoric (e.g., gesturing) and observational (e.g., listening) systems are also intimately involved. Facial expressions are a primitive type of verbal behavior. Verbal behavior is controlled by social reinforcement contingencies, with instructional and imitative variables playing a major role.

There are many verbal aspects of relaxation. Listening to and echoing instructions is common to all training methods, while the covert repetition of certain sounds or phrases is part of some. Relaxed verbal behavior is characterized by self-reports of calm and well-being. Such statements are taken as descriptions of covert events, though the social contingencies influencing self-reports must be considered. In settings requiring vocal interaction, the content of relaxed verbal behavior is relevent to the topic, and non-content aspects, such as pitch and prosody, may be characterized as calm. Unrelaxed verbal behavior includes negative self-reports, tangential content, and irregular delivery.

Visceral behavior functions to maintain the internal 'economy' of the individual. Structurally, it involves smooth and cardiac muscle and the glandular systems. Visceral behavior is controlled by reflex and respondent conditioning principles. Some systems may be controlled through operant procedures, but the mediation of other behavior modalities cannot be ruled out (Miller, 1978).

Slow and regular breathing in quiet settings is an example of overt visceral behavior generally accepted as characteristic of relaxation. In settings requiring exertion, relaxed breathing is more rapid, but deep and regular. Covert relaxed visceral behavior includes decreased heart rate and blood pressure and peripheral vasodilation; some people are able to observe these responses in themselves, but special instruments are required for accurate measurement. Unrelaxed visceral behavior involves the 'fight-or-flight' activation of various glands and smooth muscles, though the particular pattern of arousal depends on the situation and the individual. Thus, blushing, blanching, crying, and (as described in television anti-perspirant commercials) axial sweating are commonly regarded as unrelaxed visceral behavior. The role of digestive, sexual, and immune systems in relaxation is beyond the scope of this book.

Observational behavior functions to seek and select discriminative stimuli. Structurally it involves the sensory systems, often in conjunction with the motoric. Observational behavior is controlled by operant, instructional, and respondent principles.

Relaxed observational behavior is characterized by steady attending to repetitive, relatively invariant, low intensity stimuli. This is enhanced in most relaxation training settings by restricting external stimulation. Trainees are often instructed to engage in covert observational behavior, attending to interoceptive stimuli and engaging in imagery — 'seeing in the absence of the thing seen', as Skinner (1974) trenchantly describes it. Covert observational behavior is measured primarily by self-report and is difficult to verify, since there is no access to the events being observed. In settings requiring action, relaxed observational behavior involves systematic seeking and attending to task-relevant cues.

This list of relaxed behaviors is not exhaustive, but even so it is obvious that not all behaviors in all modalities occur in all settings. We use the term 'relaxed' to describe ourselves or others when we observe particular constellations of behavior in particular settings.

The Response Class of Relaxation

Relaxation may be regarded as a response class involving behavior in all four domains. A response class is made up of members which covary — the occurrence of one behavior is associated with the likelihood of increased occurrence of other behaviors. Covariation occurs both within a modality (for example, decreasing muscle tension in the jaw may also decrease tension around the eyes and forehead) and across modalities (for example, decreased muscle tension in the face may result in the verbal statement 'I feel calm').

The nature and extent of such interbehavioral control is not well understood and awaits further research. Some members may be genetically linked, as proposed by the parasympathetic theory discussed previously, in which diminished muscle tension influences visceral activity. Other links result from ontogenic experience, as when listening to the verbal description of a peaceful scene results in visual imagery. Directionality of influence is also at issue; for example, peripheral vasodilation may serve as the antecedent for the statement, 'My hands are warm,' but will repeating 'My hands are warm' affect a visceral responding?

Viewing relaxation as a response class makes explicit the assumptions of various theories and training procedures. It provides a framework for answering questions about what behaviors occur in what individuals in what settings, and with what outcomes. The following section looks at several of the most popular training procedures in terms of this behavioral taxonomy.

RELAXATION TRAINING METHODS

The taxonomy presented in the previous section provides a means of describing relaxation in common terms regardless of the particular training procedure. This section examines the antecedents and behaviors involved in several popular training procedures, looking at the similarities and differences. The clinical consequences of relaxation training will be presented in chapter 5.

Features Common to All Procedures

Benson's List. There are many features common to an array of relaxation training procedures. Benson, in keeping with his unitary theory, has proposed that there are four components to all methods, implying that these are necessary and sufficient for relaxation (Benson *et al.*, 1974). Benson's list includes: '(1) Mental Device . . . a constant stimulus . . . (2) Passive Attitude . . . One should not worry how well he is performing . . . (3) Decreased Muscle Tonus . . . a comfortable posture . . . (4) Quiet Environment . . . decreased environmental stimuli' (p. 47).

In behavioral terms, a *mental device* refers to observational behavior, which in one way or another is included in all procedures. Trainees are instructed to attend to some low-intensity event (the *constant stimulus*), such as their own breathing, proprioceptive sensations, a biofeedback signal, or the trainer's voice.

A *passive attitude* translates into verbal instructions to ignore distractions, to continue observing the 'constant stimulus', and to avoid evaluating one's performance. Such instructions are explicit in some procedures; other methods may actively evaluate and provide feedback on the trainee's progress.

Decreased muscle tonus is the explicit goal of the motoric training methods. Other procedures may not directly include this aspect, but it may be present in that trainees are generally seated in a comfortable chair.

All training is generally done in a *quiet environment*. It enhances the trainee's observation of the 'constant stimulus' and minimizes observation of distracting stimuli.

Rules for Relaxation. An additional feature common to all relaxation training methods, not mentioned by Benson, is the rationale provided to the trainee. Such a rationale may be termed the 'rules' for relaxation, since it provides a verbal statement of the contingencies for engaging in the behaviors requested by the trainer. Rules are a statement of the contingent relationships between the antecedents, behaviors, and consequences of relaxation. The trainer (or training agent, such as book or audio tape) may also include a description of the mechanism by which relaxation can produce the desired outcome. In essence the trainee is told that if she or he engages in certain behavior in certain situations, certain outcomes will occur. Such outcomes are usually delayed or accrue only after a lengthy period of practice, and an important function of a rule is to bridge the gap between behavior and consequence.

Another rule, usually implicit, is the statement: 'My approval is contingent on your following my instructions.' The trainer is seen as an expert, with special knowledge and skills, and is a potent reinforcing agent. His or her approval is an immediate consequence which keeps the trainee on task and also helps bridge the gap between relaxed behavior and its delayed benefits.

Such rules become part of the trainee's verbal repertoire, by which he or she can direct his or her own behavior in the absence of the trainer. A trainee's 'understanding' of a procedure is inferred from the degree to which he or she can repeat and follow these rules. This self-direction is seldom explicitly monitored, and is described as 'covert rules' below.

Another verbal behavior common to all methods is the self-report. The exact format varies, from rating on a numerical scale to narrative descriptions. Trainers should recognize that self-report is influenced not only by covert feelings of relaxation, but also by the social contingencies of the training situation. There may be some degree of compliance to the implied instruction, 'tell me you are relaxed.'

The effect of these general forms of instructional control, sometimes dismissed as 'placebo' or 'suggestion', is an important aspect of all relaxation training procedures. The specific instructions describing and cueing the trainee's behavior are what differentiate the various training methods. Whether or not the specific behaviors practiced in training have differential effects, above and beyond the effects of these common features, is an unresolved research question. Data exist on both sides of the issue, but numerous differences—in types and parameters of training, subject populations, dependent measures, and uncontrolled variables— prevent firm conclusions. The framework presented in this book allows a clearer focus on the relevant variables.

Distinctive Features of Relaxation Training Methods

In light of the taxonomy of behavior presented previously, it can be seen that the various relaxation training methods differ in that they emphasize particular response modalities and ignore or downplay others. Table 1.2 outlines the focus of several of the more common relaxation training procedures. While each method targets a specific response in one or two of the behavioral modalities, there usually is an implicit assumption that such training affects other responses, both within and between modalities. Each method treats relaxation as a response class, as described in the previous section, in which strengthening one member also strengthens the others.

Progressive Relaxation Training. This method emphasizes motoric behavior. Jacobson's (1938) original procedure consisted of instructions to systematically tense and relax dozens of muscle groups throughout the body, and to observe the covert sensations of tension and relaxation. Trainees received several hour-long training sessions each week for

Table 1.2. Behavioral Features of Relaxation Training Procedures*

Training method	Behavior modality			
	Motoric	Verbal	Visceral	Observational
Progressive Relaxation	Overt: Muscle tense-release. Covert: Tension.	Overt: Rules. Overt: Self-report.	—	Overt: Breathing. Covert: Proprioceptive stim.
Behavioral Relaxation	Overt: Postures. Covert: Tension.	Overt: Rules. Overt: Self-report. Covert: Labels.	Overt: Breathing.	Overt: Postures, breathing. Covert: Proprioceptive stim.
EMG Biofeedback	Covert: Tension.	Overt: Rules. Overt: Self-report.	—	Overt: Feedback signal. Covert: Proprioceptive stim.
Thermal Biofeedback	—	Overt: Rules. Overt: Self-report.	Covert: Vasodilation.	Overt: Feedback signal. Covert: Warmth.
Meditation	—	Overt: Rules. Overt: Self-report. Covert: Mantra.	Overt: Breathing.	Overt: Breathing. Covert: Mantra.
Autogenic Training	—	Overt: Rules. Overt: Self-report. Covert: Phrases.	—	Covert: Visceral and proprioceptive stim.
Hypnosis	—	Overt: Rules. Overt: Self-report.	—	Covert: Sensory and proprioceptive stimuli.
Guided Imagery	—	Overt: Rules. Overt: Self-report.	—	Covert: Sensory, proprioceptive, and visceral stimuli.

*In the case of Observational behavior, Overt and Covert refer to the event being observed.

several months, plus instructions to practice on their own a couple hours each day. Wolpe (1958) adopted an abbreviated form of Jacobson's lengthy procedure. Bernstein and Borkovec's (1973) manual has provided standardized instructions and exercises, facilitating research on this procedure. The goal of all forms is to teach observational skills, allowing the trainee to localize even slight proprioceptive stimuli of tension, and to teach motoric skills, allowing the rapid reduction of the tension. Trainees are not encouraged to verbally echo the instructions, and the common use of audiotapes for practice maintains external verbal control.

Behavioral Relaxation Training. This procedure, which is completely described in chapter 3, also emphasizes motoric behavior (Schilling & Poppen, 1983). In this case the motoric behavior is overt, allowing observation by both the trainer and trainee. This avoids the 'problem of privacy' (Skinner, 1969), in which the trainer attempts to teach discriminations of events to which he or she has no direct access. The trainee is instructed to observe his or her overt postures as well as the covert proprioceptive sensations and other feelings of relaxation. Verbal definitions and 'labels' of relaxed postures are provided, which may be covertly echoed by the trainee and employed during practice on his or her own. Visceral behavior is included as slowed breathing, and diaphragmatic breathing may also be employed.

EMG Biofeedback Training. This procedure also targets motoric behavior (Budzynski & Stoyva, 1969). In this case, the trainee alters covert muscle activity and observes the changes in a public stimulus which parallels the private event. An attempt to 'wean' the trainee from control by the external signal is sometimes made by incorporating feedback-free trials and instructing the trainee to continue whatever he or she was doing (Olton & Noonberg, 1980). In some cases the trainee may be asked to observe the covert sensations of reduced tension, but this is not always done. Generalization within the motoric response class, from the trained muscle site to other muscle groups, has been reported in some experimental investigations and has not been found in others (Qualls & Sheehan, 1981; Tarler-Benlolo, 1978). The variables responsible for general or specific effects of biofeedback training are unknown, though the use of verbal instructions has been suggested as a major factor (Qualls & Sheehan, 1981). Another factor is the fact that trainees may use the strategy of shifting their posture to achieve lowered EMG levels in the training site, which may inadvertently change EMG activity in other parts of the body (Poppen, Hanson & Ip, in press; Schilling & Poppen, 1983).

Thermal Biofeedback Training. This procedure focuses on visceral behavior, namely the dilation of peripheral vasculature (Sargent, Green, & Walters, 1973). The trainee is provided with a public signal that reflects minute changes in peripheral temperature. He or she is instructed to find some way to control the signal and to thereby control his or her vascular behavior. Although the occurrence of peripheral temperature control is well documented, disagreement remains as to whether the trainee engages in the behavior directly or first engages in behavior in another modality which mediates the vascular change (Bacon & Poppen, 1985; King & Montgomery, 1980; Miller, 1978; Olton & Noonberg, 1980; Taub & Emurian, 1976). All the response modalities have been suggested as candidates for mediating temperature control: motoric behavior, in the form of muscular relaxation (King & Montgomery, 1980); verbal behavior, in the form of autogenic phrases (Blanchard & Andrasik, 1985); visceral behavior, in the form of breathing control (Bacon & Poppen, 1985); and observational behavior, in the form of visual imagery (Blanchard & Andrasik, 1985). Biofeedback training for other visceral responses, such as heart rate, blood pressure, and skin conductance, is subject to the same considerations of mediation (Miller, 1978; Silver & Blanchard, 1978).

Meditation. This method targets verbal, visceral (breathing) and observational behavior (Benson, 1975). The trainer provides a sonorous syllable, the *mantra*, which may be alleged to have special properties or be as mundane as the word 'one'. The trainee is instructed to covertly repeat the syllable with each exhalation and to observe his or her verbal and breathing activity. Trainees are instructed to passively observe their behavior rather than actively strive to achieve some result. Since the focus is on covert behavior, the trainer must rely on public accompaniments (e.g. closed eyes, slow and regular breathing), self-report, and physiologic measures to judge progress. There exists an extensive literature supporting the effects of meditation training on decreasing muscle tension and autonomic arousal. However, a critical review of the research has asserted that such changes are no greater than those achieved by asking subjects to rest quietly (Holmes, 1984). Meditation may thus simply be a means of providing people with the social contingencies to systematically take a rest break. Indeed, proper controls for such effects are needed in all relaxation outcome research.

Autogenic Training. This procedure involves verbal and observational behavior (Schultz & Luthe, 1969). The trainer provides a series of statements concerning heaviness, warmth, and calmness in various parts of the body. The trainee covertly repeats the phrase and observes the described sensation. The statements refer to motoric and visceral activity (e.g. 'My right hand is heavy,' 'My heartbeat is calm and regular'). It assumed that such verbal and observational behavior will directly influence responding in the visceral modality, but there is little controlled research supporting such direct self-instructional control. To take a related example, repeating 'My penis is erect' is no cure for impotence. Like meditation, autogenic training may only provide a rationale for systematic rest.

Hypnosis. This procedure has been used to effect a wide variety of behaviors, including relaxation (Barber & Hahn, 1963; Paul, 1969). The trainer provides verbal descriptions of motoric and observational behavior (e.g. 'Imagine you are holding something heavy in your hand. Now the hand and arm feel heavy as if the weight were pressing down.' Weitzenhoffer & Hilgard, 1962). Unlike autogenic training, the trainee is not instructed to covertly repeat the verbal behavior, but to covertly engage in the motoric and observational behavior described. The observational behavior may include proprioceptive and visual imagery. The degree to which the trainee can be so engaged determines the success of the procedure. For example, when told that 'Your hands and arms are so heavy, like they're made of stone, that you cannot lift them,' the trainee who does not lift his or her hands when asked to do so is judged to be successfully hypnotized.

Guided Imagery. This is another verbal and observational procedure whereby the trainer describes scenes and actions in which the trainee imagines him/herself engaging (Shielkh, 1983). It differs from autogenic training and hypnosis in that trainees are instructed to construct a scene other than the training environment, such as a warm, tropical beach. They are instructed to observe the 'stimulus propositions' (Lang, 1977) of the scene in the sensory modalities of sight, sound, temperature, touch, and smell. It is similar to autogenic training and hypnosis in that trainees are instructed to attend to the 'response propositions' (Lang, 1977)—that is, their own motoric and visceral behavior, such as feeling relaxed and heavy with slow and regular pulse and breathing. As with other procedures, it is assumed that verbal and observational procedures will directly affect behavior in the visceral and motoric modalities.

Summary

Relaxation training methods include both common and specific features. Common components include a comfortable, distraction-free setting, a rationale for engaging in training, the trainer–trainee social interaction, general instructions to observe repetitive, low-intensity events, and regular practice. Specific features are the behaviors that each method targets for training. Changes in the target behaviors may be directly measured, indirectly inferred, or ignored by the trainer. (Issues in the measurement of relaxation are presented in chapter 2.) Changes in other categories of behavior, most notably visceral, are often assumed and sometimes assessed. Unresolved research questions concern the effects of training in a particular behavior modality on the other behavior within and across modalities; whether a general response class of relaxation across these modalities results from any or all of these training methods; and what effects relaxed behaviors may have on stress, pain, and anxiety problems.

Chapter Two

Assessment of Relaxation

Clinicians and researchers who employ relaxation procedures rarely bother to determine whether or not their clients and subjects actually learn the skill they so assiduously try to teach. There are two common replies to this assertion. One is that it is unimportant to do so. What is important, according to this point of view, is that the client achieve reductions in symptoms and improvement in functioning, and assessment efforts should be directed toward determining treatment outcome. This chapter first discusses the importance of measuring relaxation for determining treatment outcome.

A second response to the above assertion is that it is false. Many professionals believe that they do indeed keep track of their trainees' progress during relaxation training. This chapter also discusses the limitations of some commonly employed attempts to measure relaxation.

The main focus of this chapter is to present a method for assessing relaxation which can be easily incorporated into both clinical practice and research protocols. The Behavioral Relaxation Scale (BRS) is described, along with scoring procedures and methods for observer training. We recognize that the BRS does not provide a complete remedy, and the chapter concludes with a discussion of some issues in the multimodal assessment of relaxation.

WHY MEASURE?

The paradigm for teaching a skill involves the following steps on the part of the teacher:

1. Instruction
2. Review performance of the student

3. Reinforce progress
4. Remediate errors
5. Move to next stage of training.

Steps 3, 4, and 5 all depend on step 2, which is assessment. This much is a truism in any educational enterprise, and hardly bears repeating. However, teachers of relaxation just as routinely neglect measurement of the performance of their pupils.

As stated earlier, one reason for this neglect is the belief that such assessment is relatively unimportant. In this view, relaxation is an intermediate step and the important relation is between treatment and outcome, as shown in the diagram below.

The clinician provides a treatment—for example, autogenic training, the client experiences an outcome—for example, a reduction in headaches. This is the bread-and-butter relationship, such researchers will say, and the clinician need not be concerned about what else may be happening. An analogy may be drawn with the prescription of aspirin, whereby headache is alleviated even though the intervening mechanism of action is unknown.

Similarly, the researcher may compare Treatment X—for example, EMG biofeedback—with Treatment Y—for example, attention—placebo—with the outcome again being headache reduction. By careful control of extraneous variables, it is possible to demonstrate that the outcome is statistically more probable with Treatment X than for Treatment Y.

The researcher's concern with probabilities raises a critical point. Relationships between treatments and outcomes are never black or white. Not all persons given autogenic training improve; not all given attention–placebo fail to improve. Both clinicians and researchers are constantly seeking to improve their odds, and looking at the direct effects of training provides one means of doing so. To use the aspirin analogy, in those cases where patients fail to find relief, it is because aspirin was ineffective, because the patients failed to take the pills, or because the medication was not metabolized normally? Only by assessing the intermediate stage, the metabolites of medication, can answers be obtained and treatment odds improved. The crucial relationship is not between the *prescription* of medication and outcome but between physiologic action and outcome. Similarly, the *provision* of treatment is not the same thing as the client actually learning a skill and employing it in daily living. By assessing the client's proficiency in relaxation, it becomes possible to determine a dose–response relation, a very powerful measure of treatment effectiveness.

Another problem with looking at 'outcome' as the only dependent measure is that it is usually based on client self-report of subjective symptoms. The difficulties with this measure will be discussed in the next section. Suffice it to say here that there are many variables in addition to the 'treatment' that can influence self-report. In order to strengthen the claim of treatment effectiveness, it is important to measure what happened to the client during training while he or she is still available for objective observation. The degree of relaxation achieved in training is presumed to be a precursor of relaxation in the natural environment, which is one of the variables affecting self-report of symptoms. Thus, the assessment of relaxation gives the clinician and researcher one more handle by which to grasp the relation between treatment and outcome.

Finally, the role of assessment in training relaxation must be emphasized. Determining proficiency and providing feedback is crucial for building the client's skills. Such active guidance by the trainer goes far in enhancing the client's relaxation and improving the chances for a successful outcome.

In summary, assessment of relaxation is necessary to demonstrate treatment integrity. Providing treatment is not the same as the client receiving treatment. Determining the relationship between relaxation treatment and outcome requires that the client demonstrate that relaxation has been *learned*. In addition, assessment of relaxation allows the trainer to provide guidance, correction, and reinforcement—in short, to teach rather than merely instruct.

CURRENT MEASURES OF
RELAXATION

The assertion that professionals do not measure client behavior during training is based on reviews of the relaxation literature, which found that there is no mention of the degree to which subjects became proficient in the target behavior of relaxation (Hillenberg & Collins, 1982; Luiselli, 1980; Luiselli, Marholin, Steinman, & Steinman, 1979). Many professionals might disagree with this assessment, and insist that they do in fact measure client progress and proficiency, but in informal and indirect ways. This may well be the case, but the reliance on cursory and incomplete measures only serves to prevent the development of effective assessment tools. Some currently employed approximations to relaxation measurement are discussed in this section.

Self-Report

Self-Report of Relaxation. The widespread notion of relaxation as an internal state leads to a reliance on the client as the primary observer of that state. Consequently, the trainer may gauge the client's progress by his or her answer to the question, 'How did that go?' or 'How do you feel?' Comments by the client, such as 'I feel like I am melted in the chair' or 'I just can't seem to let myself go,' are taken as primary data on the subjective state. A related method is to arrange a more formal report system, as in systematic desensitization, where the client signals with a lifted finger that his or her state of relaxation has been disturbed (Wolpe, 1958). Another procedure is to present the client with a numbered rating scale, with associated descriptors of relaxation or arousal (Appendix C, from Schilling & Poppen, 1983).

It is necessary to include self-reports of internal events when working with verbal human clients. But such reports are not sufficient, and the relaxation trainer would do well to recognize the limitations of such behavior. The first limitation is what B.F. Skinner has called 'the problem of privacy' (Skinner, 1953). Stated simply, this problem is that people have difficulty discriminating and labeling internal stimuli because they lack corrective feedback from their environment. Little Johnny learns not to call a kitty 'doggie', or the mailman 'Daddy', when Mommy observes the error and provides corrective consequences. But such quick correction is not forthcoming in learning about internal events. We eventually arrive at a crude consensus about private stimuli through a slow process of metaphor ('I feel like a truck ran over me') and public accompaniments ('You seem down in the mouth'). But we never achieve the accuracy in discriminating such events that we do when people around us have direct access to what we are speaking about.

As an aside, we may note that the technology of biofeedback makes the client more precisely aware of internal events by allowing another observer, the therapist, to observe and label those events. For example, the therapist instructs the client, 'You are becoming more tense when the tone becomes higher in pitch, and you are relaxing when the tone becomes lower and turns off.' The therapist expresses approval when the tone decreases, and concern when it increases. The social as well as the electronic feedback is necessary for the person to learn to accurately discriminate his or her levels of tension.

Another limitation of self-report is that it is so responsive to social contingencies, often to a greater extent than to internal stimuli. It is well documented that people often report feeling more relaxed after receiving some treatment which they are told is effective, even though no change has taken place in motoric or visceral modalities (Matthews, 1971; Qualls & Sheehan, 1981; Schilling & Poppen, 1983; Reinking & Kohl, 1975). Conversely, people may report no change in feelings, even though muscle tension has actually decreased, when the procedure is labeled 'physiological assessment' rather than 'relaxation training' (e.g. Poppen *et al.*, in press). Part of the 'placebo effect' is this change in verbal behavior in response to therapist instructions and approval.

Self-Report of Symptoms. The primary dependent variable in all therapy and most research endeavors involving relaxation is the reduction of the trainee's complaint. As discussed in the previous section, this focus on outcome precludes measurement of relaxation. In some instances, such as hypertension, spasmodic torticollis, and Raynaud's disease, the disorder can be objectively measured. But in most instances, including headache, other types of pain, anxiety, and panic, the therapist must depend on the client's report. These reports may be systematically solicited, as in a Headache Diary (Blanchard & Andrasik, 1985), or more informally gathered (Well, how's it going this week?'). The limitations concerning self-report of arousal, described above, apply just as well to self-report of symptoms. Of particular concern are the social contingencies which serve to maintain such reports. For example, Fordyce (1976) has documented the influence of social contingencies on verbal reports of pain as well as other pain behaviors.

Whether the symptom is self-reported or objectively measured, the assumption is that it provides a measure of relaxation. That is, improvement in the symptom is taken to indicate that the client is successfully relaxing. In negative instances, it is not clear if the client is not engaging in relaxation or if relaxation is not having the desired effect. The latter instance merely points up a problem that is overlooked when clients do improve—namely, that the link between relaxation and headache (or panic, or back pain) is conjectural at best, and the status of the symptom does not automatically reflect the skill or frequency with which the client engages in relaxation. The relationship between relaxation and symptom change is a matter greatly in need of experimental investigation, and research that lumps the two together adds little to our knowledge of this relationship. Even the clinician, whose primary interest is in the improvement of the symptom, could provide better service if he or she knew the client's proficiency in relaxation. Such knowledge would aid the therapist in deciding whether or not to persist in relaxation training when little symptom change seems evident, and in determining which aspect of treatment to continue, or to try with other clients, when positive gains are seen.

Physiologic Measures

As discussed in chapter 1, the internal stimuli about which people are presumed to be reporting when they describe their arousal and symptoms result from the covert activity of various motoric and visceral systems. In other instances, such as hypertension, the relevant physiologic systems may exert little stimulus control over the client's verbal behavior. In either case, it would seem that a direct way of measuring relaxation is to measure physiologic activity.

Several questions immediately arise. Which physiologic systems should be measured? Under what conditions should measurement occur? How should these conditions be induced and themselves measured? What is the relationship between the conditions under which physiologic assessment can be carried out and the person's everyday living conditions? What is the reliability of such measures? How does one resolve conflicts between self-report and physiologic measures?

Which Physiologic Systems? The answer to this question involves several considerations. Foremost among these is the particular disorder for which the client is seeking treatment. In many psychophysiologic disorders, the target symptom suggests the system to be measured (Blanchard, 1981). Thus for hypertension, one would measure blood pressure, or perhaps a contributory system such as heart rate or transit time. For muscle-related pain, such as tension headache, TMJ disorder, or low back pain, EMG levels of regional musculature are appropriate. For panic attack and asthma, measures of respiration type, rate, and depth would be indicated.

Theoretical considerations are also brought to bear. For example, Benson (1975) conceptualizes relaxation in terms of diminished energy expenditure, and thus measures the body's exhaust gas, CO_2. Other autonomic theories emphasize generalized sympathetic quiescence, and measure electrodermal activity (Javel & Denholtz, 1975). Theories which emphasize motoric behavior measure EMG in one or many muscle groups (Budzynski & Stoyva, 1969; Poppen & Maurer, 1982).

Another consideration is practical, in terms of the equipment and expertise at hand. Researchers, of course, should have adequate equipment to measure the variables of interest. Clinicians may be more restricted in what is available to them. Biofeedback-based treatment has the advantage of equipment which can provide assessment of the target physiologic system, if only the trainer would bother to summarize the data from each session. When biofeedback is not employed, ethical treatment standards demand that practitioners invest in equipment and training sufficient to measure the physiologic symptoms they are targeting.

Even when narrowed by these considerations, there are literally scores of physiologic systems that present themselves for measurement. For example, a well-studied disorder such as tension headache may involve many head and neck muscles in addition to frontalis, including temporalis, masseter, orbicularis occuli, sternocleidomastoid, and cervical trapezius. Perhaps measures of blood flow in these muscles, rather than electrical activity, would be more appropriate (Olton & Noonberg, 1980). Little is known about the interrelations and influences among the multiple physiologic systems, either within a modality, such as the muscular system, or across modalities, such as the respiratory and cardiovascular systems. For example, there is considerable evidence that biofeedback-trained reduction of frontalis EMG does not influence nearby musculature (Qualls & Sheehan, 1981). On the other hand, such training is often associated with changes in cardiovascular and respiratory activity (Qualls & Sheehan, 1981). It is safe to say that our knowledge of physiologic systems in relaxation is miniscule. Rather than throwing up one's hands in despair at this chasm of ignorance, both the clinician and researcher are advised to roll up their sleeves and begin to build. By including systematic measures of physiologic activity, during relaxation training as well as pre- and post-training, in the home environment as well as in the clinic, in unusual response modalities as well as the traditional ones, the gaps in knowledge will be slowly knit together.

Under What Conditions? Physiologic measurement may be carried out in a variety of situations. If an objective of relaxation treatment is to change the activity level in a particular physiologic system, then it is necessary to measure that system while the client is engaging in relaxation. Changes in the measure from pretreatment levels over the course of training provides important feedback to the clinician, and perhaps also to the client. In the laboratory, such data provide evidence of the integrity of the independent variable and should be routinely gathered and reported.

A related objective of relaxation treatment is to reduce the arousal of a particular physiologic system under stressful conditions, or to speed recovery of the system after stress. In order to verify this objective, one can measure physiologic activity during and after some demand placed on the client. The most commonly employed laboratory stressors are 'psychological' demands, such as serial subtraction or emotional imagery, and 'physical' demands, such as the cold pressor test—placing the client's hand or foot in ice water (Blanchard, 1981). As Blanchard notes, 'This seems a very promising avenue of research but has received only limited attention thus far' (1981, p. 257). The clinical use of this technique seems limited to a few scattered reports measuring skin conductance, while the client imagines emotional scenes in systematic desensitization.

The similarity between physiologic activity in a clinic or laboratory setting and the client's everyday living situation is often assumed but rarely investigated. The underpinning of much relaxation therapy is that the physiologic changes achieved in training will be manifest in the client's natural environment. The small amount of evidence for this assumption is supportive. Agras and his associates have shown that blood pressure reductions achieved in the clinic with relaxation training persisted in the patients' work and home environments (Agras, Taylor, & Kraemer, 1980; Southam, Agras, Taylor, & Kraemer, 1982). However, home and work measures were carried out only after treatment had been completed, and hence do not show concurrence between training and generalization effects. Poppen *et al.* (in press) demonstrated that EMG reductions, accomplished with biofeedback training while students engaged in reading, concurrently generalized to their usual places of study. While these early results are promising, it is obvious that much more research needs to be done, encompassing the whole spectrum of disorders treated with the wide variety of relaxation training methods. Such research is an integral part of the task of verifying the utility of particular training methods for particular disorders.

How Reliable. Recent research has questioned the reliability of physiologic measures (Arena, Blanchard, Andrasik, Cotch, & Myers, 1983). This study of 15 young adult college students found frontalis EMG to be reliable across a variety of conditions (baseline, instructions to relax, and mental arithmetic) when assessments were performed up to one month apart. Hand temperature and heart rate were found to be similarly reliable, but only for assessments no more than a week apart. Measures of electrodermal activity, cephalic vasomotor response, and forearm flexor EMG were generally inconsistent. As the authors recognize, the implications of this research for clinical populations remain to be determined.

What is the Relationship to Other Measures? The discrepancies between physiologic measures and self-report have been noted in preceding sections. The fact that self-report is often the product of social contingencies, rather than an accurate response to internal stimuli, points up the importance of assessing multiple dimensions of relaxation. Where discrepancies arise, the trainer should be alert to what may be the important controlling stimuli for each class of behavior. Discrepancies may indicate, for example, that pain reports are controlled by social contingencies, or that inappropriate physiologic systems are being monitored. In either case, a change of treatment strategies may be indicated.

The relationship between various physiologic measures is also subject to investigation. The early classic work of John and Beatrice Lacey suggested that autonomic response classes were idiosyncratic when subjects were exposed to stressful situations (Lacey & Lacey, 1958). That is, across individuals, correlations of various measures were zero, while within each individual, stable patterns were often apparent. It is not known if this same idiosyncrasy holds for responses to relaxation training.

Measurement of Process

A common substitute for measuring relaxation itself is to count the number of training sessions. Particularly with the advent of standardized relaxation programs (e.g. Bernstein & Borkovec, 1973), researchers often simply state that the subject received X number of sessions of a particular procedure (Hillenberg & Collins, 1981). In many instances, the entire program is put on audio tape and the subject may not be observed directly. Standardized relaxation programs represent an advance, in that they allow a specification of what was done to the client in a manner that can be communicated and replicated. However, 'canned' procedures seduce the trainer into neglecting the observation of effects on the client.

A common research assumption is that when a standard, fixed number of training sessions are provided, everyone receives the same 'dose' of relaxation. However, a fixed number of sessions is no substitute for measuring the client's response to the training program. Following the medication analogy, the same dose of a drug does not produce the same blood level in all patients. Individual client differences in response to relaxation training are a well-known fact of life to researchers and clinicians. Providing only a measure of the duration of training suggests a homogeneity that can be misleading.

Some research questions may be answered by specifying a particular amount of training. For example, in comparing two or more treatment regimes in their effects on a particular disorder, it is standard operating procedure to control for amount of therapist contact by providing equal numbers of sessions, and equal session length, for all treatments. Individual differences are not of direct concern and are treated as random error variability. An alternative design would be to train subjects to a particular criterion of proficiency by different methods. The number of trials (training sessions) to criterion would provide a measure of efficacy of the various methods. Individuals who learn quickly or slowly with the various procedures could be examined in more detail for idiosyncratic variables which are related to their success or failure. Such a design is closer to clinical practice, and would provide data of interest and use to the clinician (Poppen, 1983).

We would expect clinicians to be less likely to be bound to a fixed number of relaxation training sessions and to rely more on proficiency criteria. Yet the proficiency criteria are likely to be the subjective self-reports of arousal level and symptoms discussed earlier. Clinicians also make use of audio tapes for both office training and home practice. Often the only measure of the use of these tapes is self-report in answer to the question, 'Are you practicing every day with the tape I gave you?' Advances in the technology of training delivery methods do not relieve the trainer of the responsibility of determining whether that technology is working. To borrow an example from education, do we award a student a diploma for sitting through twelve years of schooling, or for demonstrating proficiency in specific academic skills? Too often we settle for the process criterion because we have no measure of proficiency.

Informal Observation

Many clinicians, as a result of years of working with clients, are able to tell how relaxed or tense a person is, and to detect discrepancies between a client's self-report and these non-verbal cues. It is common for clients at the beginning of training to state that they are relaxed and comfortable, while the clinician can just 'see' that they are not. Similarly, a researcher may see that a subject just is not 'getting it,' despite the most assiduous administration of the relaxation protocol. What is it that the experienced trainer is responding to? Such wisdom may be difficult to communicate, and may be ascribed to 'intuition' or 'clinical acumen'.

If one closely reads the descriptions provided by the pioneers in relaxation, such as Wolpe (1958; 1973), Bernstein and Borkovec (1973), and particularly Jacobson (1938), one finds clues as to what features of the client the clinician is responding to. This is getting close to the heart of behavioral relaxation assessment. Our basic premise is that the client emits certain behavior that tells the observer how relaxed or aroused he or she is. The following section describes the nature of these relaxed behaviors.

Summary. Several approximate measurements of the complex behavior called relaxation exist in the clinic and the laboratory. These include self-report, physiologic assessment, process measurement, and informal observation. But systematic efforts to monitor the progress of trainees are rare. This state of affairs may exist because trainers accept the current measurement procedures as sufficient, and because no good alternative is available. The preceding sections have described the shortcomings of current measurement procedures. The following section presents a different procedure for assessing relaxation, which, while not solving all the problems, offers the clinician and the researcher an easy method for measuring the motoric domain.

—1

THE BEHAVIORAL RELAXATION
SCALE (BRS)

In the previous sections of this chapter, measurement of the presumed internal state of relaxation has been discussed. Primarily, self-report has been used to measure a covert, undifferentiated 'state' of relaxation, and physiologic recording has been used to measure covert motoric and visceral aspects of this state. The basic premise of the BRS is that a relaxed person engages in overt motoric behavior that is characteristic of relaxation. It is possible for an external observer to take note of these behaviors and to judge how relaxed the client is. At this point, the concern is only with relaxation in the training situation. In later sections, the issue of relaxation assessment in other types of situations will be addressed. Also, the BRS is primarily a measure of the motoric behavior aspects of relaxation. A more complete multimodal assessment procedure will conclude this chapter.

A Brief History of the BRS

As one reads the classic work of Edmund Jacobson, one is struck by the descriptive detail of what to look for in his patients. His text is accompanied by many photographs, showing the trainer what the outcome of his efforts should look like. Similarly, other investigators have presented phenomenological descriptions of what transpires as a person becomes relaxed, along with hints on how to assess it. Wolpe (1958; 1973) and Bernstein and Borkovec (1973) have been particularly helpful in this respect. The contributions of Arnold Lazarus, who instructed the author in the arcane art of relaxation, should also be acknowledged. Many years of teaching relaxation, as well as teaching students to teach relaxation, resulted in some 'rules of thumb' for assessing relaxation.

Don Schilling was the first to apply these rules of thumb, when he undertook relaxation training with 'pre-delinquent' boys. Progressive relaxation training had resulted in boys who were good at the 'tensing' part but poor at 'releasing'. Showing some creative behaviorism, Don decided to teach the boys to 'look relaxed'. Sure enough, the children not only could look relaxed, they reported that they felt relaxed, and exhibited a calm demeanor after each session. All that remained was to work out a specific list of behaviors and to formally test the reliability of observation and the relation to other measures. That list is known as the BRS.

Ten Relaxed Behaviors

The BRS consists of a description of ten postures and activities characteristic of a fully relaxed person whose body is fully supported by a
reclining chair or similar device. First, these behaviors are described in
word and picture. Next, a method for systematically observing them will
be presented.

Each behavior consists of an overt posture or activity of a particular
region of the body. In order to enhance discrimination, both relaxed and
some commonly occurring unrelaxed behaviors are presented for each
item.

1: Head

Relaxed. The head is motionless and supported by the recliner with the
nose in the midline of the body. Body midline can usually be determined
by clothing features such as shirt buttons or apex of V neckline. Part of the
nostrils and the underside of the chin are visible. See Figure 2.1-A.

Unrelaxed. (a) Movement of the head. (b) Head turned from body
midline; the entire nose is beyond midline (Fig. 2.1-B). (c) Head tilted
downward; the nostrils and underside of the chin are not visible (Fig.
2.1-B). (d) Head unsupported by the recliner (Fig. 2.1-C). (e) Head tilted
upward; the entire underside of the chin is visible (Fig. 2.1-D).

2: Eyes

Relaxed. The eyelids are lightly closed with a smooth appearance and no
motion of the eyes beneath the lids. See Figure 2.2-A.

Unrelaxed. (a) Eyes open. (b) Eyelids closed but wrinkled or fluttering
(Fig. 2.2-B). (c) Eyes moving under the lids.

3: Mouth

Relaxed. The lips are parted at the center of the mouth from one-quarter
to one inch (7 to 25 mm), with the front teeth also parted. See Figure 2.3-A.

Unrelaxed. (a) Teeth in occlusion. (b) Lips closed (Fig. 2.3-B). (c) Mouth
open greater than one inch (25 mm); in most cases the corners of the
mouth will separate when the mouth is open beyond criterion (Fig.
2.3-C). (d) Tongue motion, e.g. licking lips.

4: Throat

Relaxed. Absence of motion. See Figure 2.4.

Unrelaxed. Any movement in the throat and neck, e.g. swallowing or
other larynx action, twitches in the neck muscles.

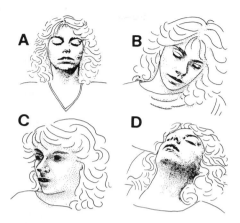

FIGURE 2.1. Postures of the head: A = relaxed;
B, C, and D = unrelaxed.

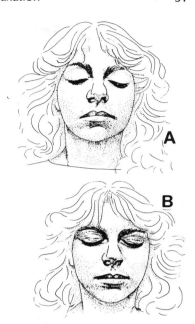

FIGURE 2.2. Postures of the eyes:
A = relaxed; B = unrelaxed.

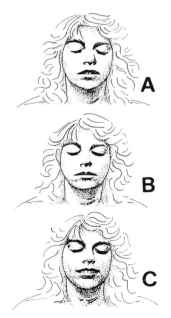

FIGURE 2.3. Postures of the mouth:
A = relaxed; B and C = unrelaxed.

FIGURE 2.4. Relaxed posture of the throat.

5: Shoulders

Relaxed. Both shoulders appear rounded and transect the same horizontal plane. They rest against the recliner with no motion other than respiration. See Figure 2.5-A.

Unrelaxed. (a) Movement of shoulders. (b) Shoulders on a diagonal plane (Fig. 2.5-B). (c) Shoulders are raised or lowered so as not to appear rounded (Fig. 2.5-C).

6: Body

Relaxed. The body is relaxed when the torso, hips, and legs are symmetrical around midline, resting against the chair, with no movement. See Figure 2.6-A.

Unrelaxed. (a) Any movement of the torso, excluding respiration. (b) Twisting of torso, hips, or legs out of midline (Fig. 2.6-B). (c) Any movement of the hips, legs, or arms, which does not result in movement of feet or hands (these are scored separately). (d) Any part of the back, buttocks, or legs not supported by the recliner.

7: Hands

Relaxed. Both hands are resting on the armrest of the chair or on the lap, with palms down and the fingers curled in a claw-like fashion. The fingers are sufficiently curled if a pencil can pass freely beneath the highest point of the arc (excluding the thumb). See Figure 2.7-A.

Unrelaxed. (a) Hands gripping the armrest. (b) Fingers extended and straight (Fig. 2.7-B). (c) Fingers curled so that nails touch the surface of the armrest (Fig. 2.7-C). (d) Fingers intertwined. (e) Movement of the hands.

8: Feet

Relaxed. The feet are pointed away from each other at an angle between 60 and 90 degrees. See Figure 2.8-A.

Unrelaxed. (a) Movement of feet. (b) Feet pointing vertically or at angle less than 60 degrees (Fig. 2.8-B). (c) Feet pointing out at an angle greater than 90 degrees (Fig. 2.8-C). (d) Feet crossed at the ankles (Fig. 2.8-D). (e) One heel placed more than one inch (25 mm) fore or aft of the other.

9: Quiet

Relaxed. No vocalizations or loud respiratory sounds.

Unrelaxed. Any verbalization or vocalization, such as talking, sighing, grunting, snoring, gasping, coughing.

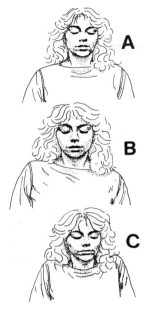

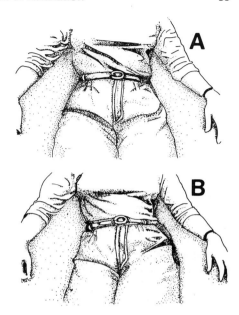

FIGURE 2.5. Postures of the shoulders:
A = relaxed; B and C = unrelaxed.

FIGURE 2.6. Postures of the body:
A = relaxed; B = unrelaxed.

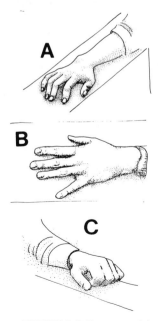

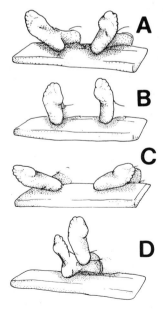

FIGURE 2.7. Postures of the hands:
A = relaxed; B and C = unrelaxed.

FIGURE 2.8. Postures of the feet:
A = relaxed; B, C, and D = unrelaxed.

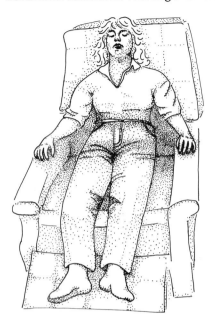

FIGURE 2.9. Full view of all relaxed postures.

10: Breathing

Relaxed. The breath frequency is less than that observed during baseline, with no breathing interruptions. One breath equals one complete inhale–exhale cycle. A breath is counted if any part of the inhale occurs on the cue starting the observation interval and any part of the exhale occurs on the cue ending the observation interval (see section on observational recording.

Unrelaxed. (a) Breath frequency is equal to or greater than that during baseline. (b) Any irregularity that interrupts the regular rhythm of breathing, such as coughing, laughing, yawning, sneezing, and so forth.

All relaxed behaviors are shown together in Figure 2.9. The trainee can be scanned from head to feet on a systematic basis in order to measure relaxation, as presented in the next section.

Using the Behavioral Relaxation Scale

One of the main uses of the BRS is to assess the degree of relaxation attained by a client participating in a particular relaxation training procedure. As chapter 3 describes, the BRS is an integral part of a relaxation training method called Behavioral Relaxation Training. However, the

BRS is useful by itself as a dependent measure for any relaxation training procedure chosen by the trainer. In its standard form, the BRS requires that the training be carried out with the trainee seated in a reclining chair or similar device. Modifications for use with the client seated in a straight back chair will be presented later.

Duration of the Observation Period. The BRS requires an observation period, usually at the conclusion of a relaxation training session. It may also be employed at the beginning of a session as a pre-treatment measure. The duration of the observation period must be several minutes. We have employed durations of 3, 5, and 10 minutes. The longer the period, the more representative sample of relaxed behavior will be obtained. But considerations of time constraints and trainee characteristics are important and should be evaluated for each application. Five minutes is sufficient for most purposes.

Each minute of the observation period is divided into three intervals: a 30-second interval to observe breathing rate, a 15-second interval to observe the other nine items on the BRS, and a 15-second interval to record the observations on the BRS Score Sheet. The BRS Score Sheet is included as Appendix A. Copies of the BRS Score Sheet should be made for the trainer to use in assessing relaxation.

Reactivity. Any behavioral observation procedure may be reactive if the person is aware of the observation. That is, the act of measurement may influence the behavior being measured, resulting in inaccurate assessment. We have found two major areas of reactivity in employing the BRS, which the user should be aware of and take steps to reduce. The two reactive features of the BRS are the discriminability of the observation period and the 'being watched' phenomenon.

The discriminability of the observation period is an important factor in gathering accurate measures. Usually, it is desirable to measure relaxation in the absence of other interactions with the client. Observation is typically carried out in silence, which may provide a cue to the client about a change in conditions. That is, if relaxation training has employed some sort of signal or instruction administered to the client, as in biofeedback or progressive muscle relaxation, and this presentation suddenly ends, the client may be alerted that the session is about to end. This could disrupt relaxation. We typically instruct clients that at the conclusion of training they will be asked to relax 'on their own' for several minutes while we assess the effectiveness of training; they are instructed to continue whatever they have been doing in training until we tell them the session is over. This is sufficient for most people. However, we have found in working with hyperactive children (chapter 4) that it is necessary to allow a couple of minutes at the conclusion of training for the children to 'settle down' before collecting relaxation measures. It is also possible to incorporate an observation period within the training session, or to continue to administer treatment until the end of the session, so that there are no changes to alert the client.

Concerns about being watched is another reactive aspect of the BRS. This problem, while not widespread, is most evident in the initial stages of research, when baseline measures are being collected. It is at this time that the procedures are the most unfamiliar to the subject, and also the time when the subject is most likely to have his or her eyes open, watching the trainer watch him or her. This can be particularly unnerving. 'Eyes closed' is one of the items on the BRS, and instructions to the subject to close his or her eyes would be a confound in the baseline period of a research project. In clinical practice, where baseline data collection is usually not so rigorous, it does no harm to ask the client to close his or her eyes; this merely inflates the baseline relaxation score by 10% and can be noted accordingly.

In addition, all trainees should be instructed in the rationale given at the start of their training procedure that it is necessary to measure the effects of the training, and that they will therefore be observed. The emphasis should be that it is the training procedure which is being measured, rather than how well the trainee is performing, in order to avoid undue performance pressure. Examples of such instructions will be given in a later section. Generally, the trainee becomes more at ease as training progresses and observation is accepted as part of the procedure.

Where facilities permit, it is possible to observe the trainee through a one-way window or to use a video camera to view or record an observation period. Not seeing the observer may put the trainee more at ease. When this is done, ethical practice requires that the person be informed that observation is taking place. In all cases, either clinical or research, every effort should be made to establish good rapport between trainer and trainee and to assure him or her that confidentiality is always maintained.

Setting. The observer should place himself or herself in a position so as to obtain a full and unobstructed view of the trainee. Since symmetry around midline is an important aspect of several items on the BRS, the observer should not be seated completely to one side of the trainee. In order to best observe symmetry, the observer may sit at the foot of the chair, directly facing the trainee. However, if the client's feet are elevated, the feet may block the observer's view of 'Breathing', 'Body', or 'Hands'. Also, if the trainee is wearing a skirt, such a position may seem improper. We have found that placing the observer to one side of the foot of the recliner, at the '5 o'clock' or '7 o'clock' positions, provides a good view of symmetry and all behaviors listed on the BRS. The observer should be seated about one meter from the trainee. The room should be lighted well enough to permit observation of small movements, but no so brightly so as to disrupt relaxation. All the above considerations are especially important in the placement of a video camera or a one-way window, which tend to restrict observation.

Scoring the BRS. The observer requires a timing device to divide each minute of the observation period into appropriate scoring intervals. One option is to use an electronic stopwatch attached to a clipboard holding the BRS Score Sheet. Older model stopwatches, which make a click when started and a loud ticking when running, may be intrusive and are not recommended. When using a stopwatch, the observer must be careful not to avert his or her eyes from the client and perhaps miss the occurrence of unrelaxed behavior. Alternatively, an easily read clock, with a sweep second hand or digital readout of seconds, may be placed just behind the client, allowing the observer to view the clock as he or she scans the client. Another good method is to put time cues on an audio cassette tape, which then can be played by the observer and heard unobtrusively through a small plug-type earphone.

Before starting the observation period, the observer should write in the client's name or identification code on the BRS Score Sheet (Appendix A). The date, time, session number, and other relevant training data should also be written in. The client's baseline breathing rate, determined from pre-training baseline sessions, should be written in the box at the top of the BRS Score Sheet. The method used to determine a person's baseline breathing rate is described in a later section.

BRS scoring involves an interval recording method of behavioral observation. The presence or absence of a particular event during a specified interval of time is recorded; occurrences outside that specified interval are ignored.

The first behavior scored in each interval is Breathing. With the onset of each minute of the observation period, the observer determines whether or not the client is inhaling. If so, the observer counts this as the start of an inhale–exhale cycle; if not, the observer waits until the next inhale before beginning counting. Each inhale–exhale cycle is counted as one breath. When the timing device indicates that 30 seconds have elapsed, the observer stops counting breaths. If the client is exhaling at the end of the breathing observation interval, the cycle is counted as a complete breath. If the client is inhaling at the end of the interval, that breath is not counted. The observer writes the number of breaths in the box at the top of each column of the BRS Score Sheet, opposite 'Breathing'. If an interruption to breathing occurs (see behavioral descriptions) mark an 'X' in the box.

For the next 15 seconds of each minute, the observer scans the client for any unrelaxed behavior in the other nine items listed on the BRS. If an unrelaxed behavior is observed, the observer silently repeats the one-word label for that behavior to him or herself to aid recall until the end of the interval. If recall is a problem, the observer may immediately circle the minus sign in the appropriate column of the BRS Score Sheet, opposite the particular item noted. This should be done quickly so as not to miss other occurrences of unrelaxed behavior.

For the final 15 seconds of each minute, the observer circles the minus signs in the appropriate column, opposite the labels for any unrelaxed behaviors observed in the preceding 15-second interval. If no unrelaxed behaviors were noted, the appropriate plus signs are circled. The breathing rate written in the small box at the top of each column is compared to the baseline breathing rate. If the rate is less than baseline, the plus sign is circled; if the rate is equal to or greater than baseline, or if an interruption occurred, the minus sign is circled.

This process is repeated for each successive minute of the observation period.

The BRS score for each observation period is a percentage based on the number of behaviors scored as relaxed or unrelaxed, divided by the total number of observations. The number of relaxed behaviors is the total number of plus signs that were circled; the number of unrelaxed behaviors is the number of minus signs circled. If a five-minute observation period is employed, the total number of observations is 50 (5 minutes × 10 behaviors); if a ten-minute period is employed, the total number of observations is 100. The BRS may be scored in either a negative (percent unrelaxed) or positive (percent relaxed) direction. 'Percent unrelaxed' is the total number of minus signs divided by the total number of observations; 'percent relaxed' is the total number of plus signs divided by the total number of observations. We have used the negative scoring to show a decline in unrelaxed behavior parallel to decreases in muscle tension (Schilling & Poppen, 1983). Positive scoring shows progress in a fashion more easily understood by the client. The trainer should choose a scoring method that best serves the requirements of the particular training situation.

Baseline Breathing Rate. A baseline breathing rate must be established as the standard against which further breathing rates are measured. It is important to observe a sufficient number of intervals in order to obtain a representative sample of breathing rates. For research studies, we recommend a minimum of three five-minute observation periods, a total of 15 measurement intervals. In clinical settings, it may be useful to employ a single baseline session of at least 15 minutes, in which the client is told to relax as he or she normally does.

During baseline observation sessions, Breathing is scored as described above. The mean rate is then calculated by summing all the individual rates for each interval and dividing by the total number of observations.

Intervals which were scored as 'interruptions' are not included in calculating the mean breathing rate. All fractional values for the mean breathing rate are 'rounded up' to the next whole number. This value is then entered in the box at the top of the BRS Score Sheet as the 'Baseline Breathing Rate'.

The astute reader will have observed that the BRS score for baseline sessions cannot be calculated until after a baseline breathing rate has been determined. Once the baseline breathing rate has been established, the BRS score for baseline sessions can then be calculated in the same way that it is for other sessions.

Training BRS Observers

The trainer wishing to use the BRS must be able to do so easily and accurately. Ease of use allows the BRS to be unobtrusively incorporated into the relaxation training routine. Accuracy is essential to make sure that the BRS does the job it is intended to do. In addition, when the BRS is employed in research settings, it is important to demonstrate that it is scored reliably—that is, that two or more observers observe and report the same events. In this regard, Boice (1983) has reported that investigators employing behavioral observation routinely fail to evaluate the competence of their observers. Simply requiring observers to produce similar reports does not insure accuracy or reliability. Training observers is itself an issue in behavioral technology (Johnston & Pennypacker, 1980).

On its face, the BRS appears straightforward and simple to learn and use. But this simplicity should not mislead the user into assuming that no background and training is necessary. It does, however, make such training relatively easy to accomplish. We have found the following training protocol, based on behavioral technology principles (Hartmann & Wood, 1984; Johnston & Pennypacker, 1980), to be effective in training clinical and research observers to accurately and reliably use the BRS.

Memorize the BRS Items. First, the observers must master the definitions of each of the ten relaxed behaviors and the commonly seen unrelaxed behaviors, presented earlier in this chapter. In addition, the use of the BRS Score Sheet must be learned.

BRS Written Criterion Test. After memorizing the items, observers should pass a written test covering all BRS items. Observers are required to define the items and provide examples of relaxed and unrelaxed behaviors for each. Sample tests are provided in Appendix B. A 100% criterion of proficiency is recommended before proceeding with training. Otherwise, trainees should repeat steps 1 and 2.

Analog Relaxation Observation. Observers are now ready to score the items of the BRS with a live or videotaped model. If facilities permit, and many observers need to be trained, it is useful to construct a videotape which provides a standardized sequence of behaviors to be scored.

Individual Items. For successive 30-second intervals, the observer monitors a single item of the BRS and scores it as relaxed or unrelaxed. A predetermined sequence of items is followed. The model (live or video-taped) emits relaxed behavior during a random 50% of the intervals and various unrelaxed behaviors during the other 50%. In addition to learning discrimination of the behaviors, this procedure trains the observer to keep track of time while observing the client. Practice should continue until 100% proficiency is achieved.

Multiple Items. A five-minute observation period is employed, in which the observer scores successive one-minute intervals for all ten items on the BRS, using the Score Sheet. The model displays a predetermined sequence of relaxed and unrelaxed behaviors. Videotapes are particularly useful at this stage, in that a series of five-minute scenes can be employed, and the observer's scores compared to the predetermined standard. If the scenes are done live, the model must be skillful in following the predeter-mined sequence, so that questions do not arise as to whether the model or the observer was responsible for a disagreement. If live observation is employed, it is best to have a trained primary observer simultaneously score the intervals and serve as a standard of comparison. Each of the 50 cells in the BRS Score Sheet for a five-minute observation period are compared with the standard, and disagreements are explained. A video-tape is useful in this regard because an interval in question can be replayed and differences in opinion resolved.

Live Relaxation Observation. If videotape has been employed in the previous step, observation of a live model is now necessary. Comparisons of the observer's BRS scoring with that of a trained primary observer are carried out, and a reliability score is calculated, based on the 50 cells in the BRS Score Sheet. Reliability is expressed as a percentage in which the number of agreements between the two observers is divided by 50. Training should continue until reliability is consistently 90% or better. Disagreements should be discussed and clarified.

Client Observation. The observer can now score an actual client in conjunc-tion with another trained observer. Permission to include another observer should be obtained from the client, along with the straight-forward explanation that the new observer is learning clinical procedures. Agreement between observers should be 85% or better. The observer is now ready to serve as an independent or primary observer.

Recalibration. Many authors recommend that observers periodically undergo a check of their observation skills during the course of a project, in order to guard against observer drift (Hartmann & Wood, 1984). Observers can occasionally be cycled through the previous two steps for this purpose.

In conclusion, researchers and practitioners are encouraged to evaluate the effectiveness of this or any observer training program. In addition, research reports should include the results of such evaluations, and a description of observer training procedures with sufficient detail for replication.

Validation of the Behavioral Relaxation Scale

Validation of an assessment device requires the demonstration of correspondence between scores on that device and some other accepted criterion of behavior. The BRS has been validated in two ways, procedurally and concurrently. In the first instance, generally accepted relaxation procedures produced significant changes on the BRS while a credible placebo procedure did not (Schilling & Poppen, 1983). In the second instance, relaxed and unrelaxed behaviors, as defined by the BRS, were related to tension levels in relevant muscle groups (Poppen & Maurer, 1982). These studies are described in more detail below.

Procedural Validation. Schilling and Poppen (1983) trained groups (n = 8) of young adult volunteers in four 'stress reduction' procedures: frontalis EMG biofeedback, progressive relaxation training, Behavioral Relaxation Training (BRT, described in chapter 3), and a music placebo. Everyone received seven training sessions, plus pre- and post-training assessments. Biodfeedback consisted of individually administered auditory feedback for changes in frontalis tension. Progressive relaxation training consisted of individually administered audio-tape tense–release exercise instructions (Bernstein & Borkovec, 1973). Music consisted of taped presentations of music marketed as a stress-reduction aid, along with attention-focusing instructions.

The important finding was that each of the relaxation procedures — progressive relaxation, biofeedback, and BRT — resulted in statistically significant changes in the BRS, while the placebo procedure did not. These effects are seen in Figure 2.10. People trained in three different relaxation procedures decreased the amount of unrelaxed motoric behavior, while those in placebo condition showed no change.

Independent verification of this finding has been reported. Luiselli (1980) described a Relaxation Checklist, similar in some respects to the BRS. He reported that significant increases in relaxed behavior occurred

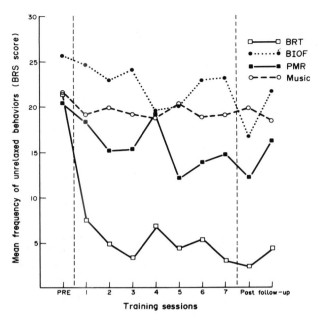

FIGURE 2.10. Behavioral Relaxation Scale scores for four training procedures: Behavioral Relaxation Training (BRT), Frontalis EMG Biofeedback (BIO), Progressive Muscle Relaxation (PMR), and Music Placebo (MUS). From 'Behavioral Relaxation Training and Assessment', by D.J. Schilling and R. Poppen, 1983, *Journal of Behavior Therapy and Experimental Psychiatry*, *14*, pp. 99–107. Copyright 1983 Pergamon Press Inc. Used with permission.

on this Checklist for college students who received a single progressive relaxation training session, compared to persons receiving a control procedure.

Blanchard and colleagues (1986a), as part of a hypertension treatment program, reported that patients receiving eight progressive relaxation training sessions achieved an average of 84% relaxed behaviors on the BRS for their last four training sessions. Unfortunately, neither pre-treatment BRS measures nor BRS measures for patients in a thermal biofeedback group were collected. In a later report, this research group found that BRS scores steadily improved as training progressed (Wittrock, Blanchard, & McCoy, in press).

Concurrent Validation. The BRS can also be validated by looking for correlated changes in other members of the relaxation response class. Schilling and Poppen (1983) found significant correlations between measures of frontalis EMG and BRS, particularly in the BRT and the biofeedback groups. There was little relationship between self-report and

BRS, in that most people reported themselves as improving regardless of their score on other measures.

In a direct validation study, Poppen and Maurer (1982) measured EMG levels in the muscles anatomically related to the postures described in the BRS. Six male volunteers, aged 23 to 27 years, served as subjects. EMG measurements were collected as the subjects engaged in the relaxed or unrelaxed postures for 5-minute periods. Subjects were not instructed to 'tense' or 'relax', but were instructed and guided into the postures as topographically described in the BRS.

The mean EMG levels for nine muscle groups, as subjects engaged in relaxed and unrelaxed postures, are shown in Figure 2.11. In all instances, relaxed postures were significantly lower than unrelaxed postures. Relaxed EMG levels are indicated by the squares, while unrelaxed levels are indicated by circles and triangles.

Tension levels in the forearm extensors are shown in the top left panel of Figure 2.11. Tension in this muscle group was equally elevated while subjects extended (triangles) or flexed (circles) their fingers. Similarly, tension in the forearm flexors, shown in the top middle panel of Figure 2.11, was elevated in both extended (triangles) and flexed (circles) unrelaxed postures.

Tension levels for a unilateral sternocleidomastoid placement are shown in the top right panel of Figure 2.11. EMG levels while the head was rotated in a contralateral direction, to the side opposite the electrode placement (triangles), were greater than those during ipsilateral rotation (circles).

Tension levels in the gracillis muscle group of the upper thigh are shown in the center left panel of Figure 2.11. Tension was higher when the feet were parallel, with the toes pointed up (triangles), than when the toes were pointed out at greater then 90° (circles). The opposite was true for the vastus muscle group, shown in the center middle panel of Figure 2.11.

Tension levels in the trapezius were elevated when the shoulders were slightly raised, as shown in the center right panel of Figure 2.11.

Tension in the suprahyoid muscles of the throat, shown in the bottom left panel of Figure 2.11, was increased while the subject engaged in one-minute intervals of: (a) talking; (b) coughing; (c) swallowing; (d) 'clearing the throat'; (e) humming.

Tension in the masseter muscle of the jaw, shown in the bottom middle panel of Figure 2.11, was elevated while the subject (a) placed his lips and teeth together, and increased even more when the subject (b) engaged in smiling.

Tension in the canthus area of the eye was elevated when the eyes were open, as shown by the triangles in the bottom right panel of Figure 2.11.

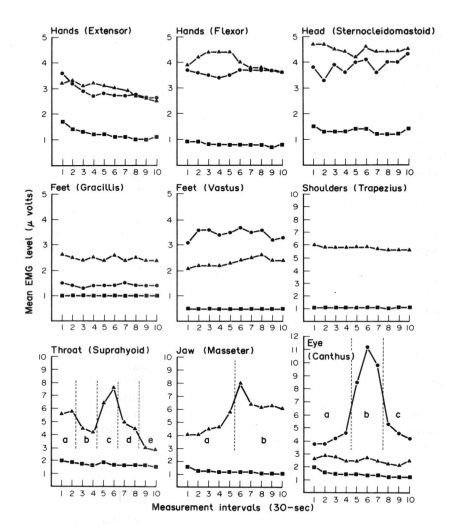

FIGURE 2.11. Mean EMG levels for nine muscle groups in either relaxed (squares) or unrelaxed (circles and triangles) postures. See text for description of postures. From 'Electromyographic Analysis of Relaxed Postures', by R. Poppen and J. Maurer, 1982, *Biofeedback and Self-Regulation, 7*, pp. 491–498. Copyright 1982 Plenum Publishing Corp. Used with permission.

This figure also shows that tension increased even more when the eyelids were closed (circles) but: (a) fluttering, (b) squeezed, and (c) eyes moving.

This study effectively dissected the BRS, showing that each element is intimately related to tension levels in particular muscle groups. Thus when a person assumes a relaxed posture, it is likely that tension in the associated muscle groups markedly decreases. As people undergo relaxation training, by whatever procedure, and learn to minimize tension throughout their bodies, this is reflected by the relaxed behaviors defined by the BRS.

The relationship between the BRS and the visceral measure of blood pressure (BP) was determined by Wittrock *et al.* (in press). BRS ratings were positively correlated with in-session systolic BP in the final two training sessions. However, the BRS scores were not related to criterion measures of 'success' or 'failure' in BP reduction one month after training. Interestingly, self-ratings of relaxation were related to the success/failure criterion, did not show consistent improvement over time, and were related to BP measures in the final two training sessions. No correlations between BRS and self-ratings were computed, though from their differing relationships to other measures one would not expect much. It should be noted that the BRS scores in this study were based on one-shot ratings rather than time-sampled observations, and no reliability of measurement was obtained.

Summary. The BRS has been shown to change in the expected direction when people undergo relaxation training in the motoric domain, namely progressive relaxation training, frontalis EMG biofeedback, and, of course, BRT. Moreover, tension in the relevant musculature is closely related to relaxed and unrelaxed postures as defined by the BRS. The relationships between BRS and scores in other behavior domains have not been extensively researched.

MULTIMODAL ASSESSMENT

As described in chapter 1, relaxation is a complex behavior, involving responses in the motoric, visceral, verbal, and observational behavior modalities. Relaxation training is assumed to produce behavior change in all of these modes. Assessment of relaxation should reflect this complexity. Since there are no universally accepted assessment procedures for each of these modalities, the trainer will have to make his or her own judgments and selections. This section offers some guidelines in making those selections.

Motoric Behavior

The Behavioral Relaxation Scale is an observational procedure providing a reliable, valid, quantified measure of the motoric aspects of relaxation. The BRS is easily learned and can be incorporated into clinical practice or research protocols with minimal disruption. It provides an ongoing measure of progress, which should be useful to both the trainer and the trainee. Unlike EMG and other physiologic measures, which are idiosyncratic to the particular electronic device employed, it provides a standardized metric, allowing easy communication between trainers and researchers in different settings.

EMG recording is a measure of motoric behavior that is regularly employed, most commonly in clinical and research settings that utilize EMG biofeedback. Frontalis EMG is the most widely employed and the most widely criticized measure (e.g., Qualls & Sheehan, 1981; Surwit & Keefe, 1978). There are questions concerning the relationship between frontalis tension and tension in other muscles, and about its relationship to the client's symptoms. These same questions can be raised about any placement site. Also, the unit of EMG measurement (voltage) is not comparable across devices and is not easily understood by some trainees. Other difficulties with EMG recording include the expense of electronic equipment purchase and maintenance, the intrusiveness of wires, electrodes, and gel, the necessity to transform the data to some useful format, and the shortage of competent technicians.

Given the shortcomings of EMG measurement and the availability of an alternative in the BRS, is there a place for EMG in the assessment of relaxation? As a measure of overall, generalized relaxation, the shortcomings of single-site EMG recording appear to outweigh its usefulness. However, in cases where the purpose of treatment is to reduce muscle tension in a particular body site or muscle group, either through EMG biofeedback or some other technique, then it is incumbant on the trainer to demonstrate that such changes actually occurred. That is, in cases where the presumed mechanism of action is muscle tension, such as tension headache, myofacial pain/dysfunction, or low-back pain, it is not sufficient to assume that decreases in pain reports accurately reflect muscle tension reduction. Good practice, as well as any contribution to our knowledge of relaxation, requires that activity in the suspected muscle sites be measured and related to the treatment procedure. This will assure the trainer (and the trainee) that the procedures employed are appropriate, or, in negative instances, that some other site, treatment, or formulation of the problem is in order.

Visceral Behavior

Many of the difficulties with EMG recording apply similarly to measurements of visceral behavior. No single measure of autonomic activity will provide an index of the visceral component of relaxation, much less a measure of a global state. The expense, complexity, and intrusiveness of visceral measurement often exceed that of EMG recording. And visceral measures are subject to many additional vagaries that limit their usefulness, such as individual idiosyncrasies in arousal patterns, reactivity to external stimuli (e.g. room temperature, noise), and reactivity to other behavior (e.g. movement, respiration).

Nevertheless, when the goal of relaxation training is to effect a change in a particular visceral system, it is necessary to document that change. This applies not only to those cases where the visceral behavior is the problem (e.g., hypertension, Raynaud's phenomenon), but also where it is the hypothesized mechanism of action (e.g., the vasomotor system in migraine, the respiratory system in panic attack). Gratuitous physiologizing may impress a naive client, but in the long run it does not advance the scientific status of relaxation training.

Verbal Behavior

The verbal component of relaxation is primarily a function of two factors: internal events and external social contingencies, with the latter often exerting the stronger control. Assessments of verbal behavior typically assume the former and neglect the latter. Separation of these two classes of verbal behavior may be difficult, and has rarely been attempted. Yet, to gather an accurate measure of relaxation, trainers need to consider both classes.

At the simplest level, different questions can be asked of the trainee in order to measure each verbal class. First of all, the trainee may be taught to discriminate these two verbal response classes by means of instructions. He or she can be told directly that people often respond to questions about how they feel in terms of the situation and what they think their audience wants to hear. Examples can be given, in which the reply to the question 'How do you feel?' would differ depending on whether the questioner was a casual acquaintance, a doctor, a parent, or a TV reporter. The trainee can be asked to describe his or her own examples to make sure he or she understands the concept of social contingency control. Then the trainee can be instructed to think of him or herself as a private audience, and to answer the question 'How do you feel?' as accurately as possible. With this instructional history, relaxation can be assessed by asking the trainee 'How relaxed do you think your trainer wants you to say you are?' and 'How relaxed do you tell yourself you are?' For each, a rating scale such as that in Appendix C, may be useful. It may also be useful to supply a list of adjectives to be selected or rated, such as 'heavy,' 'warm,' 'calm,' 'floating,' for both the social and private audience. By recognizing and accepting social contingencies in a matter-of-fact way, it may be possible to teach the trainee to make finer discriminations of private events and to more accurately report them.

Observational Behavior

Most relaxation training procedures ask the trainee to covertly engage in observation. Guided imagery, which targets this mode of behavior, attempts to measure it by asking the trainee to report whether or not he or she engaged in the requested behavior and to rate the 'clarity' or 'vividness' of the image achieved. Much more could be done. Assessment could include asking people to describe the imagined scene and scoring their description according to the number and variety of details, perhaps analogous to a Rorschach protocol.

A minimal level of observational behavior assessment entails asking the client to describe or rate the events which were observed while engaging in the relaxation procedure. For example, in biofeedback procedures the client is asked to observe an external auditory or visual signal. This could be assessed by asking the client to describe the signal and the relation between it and his or her behavior. In progressive relaxation training, the client is asked to observe kinesthetic cues in the muscles and joints; in autogenic training, the client is asked to observe sensations of warmth, coolness, and heaviness in various body parts. Assessment would consist of descriptions and ratings of the location, nature, and intensity of these events. Numerical scales and adjective lists would provide structure for such assessments. Verbal report is necessarily the means of assessing any covert observational behavior. Thus, the concerns about social contingency control of verbal behavior apply in this case also.

CONCLUSIONS

Although relaxation training methods have been employed for centuries, the status of relaxation as a scientific variable is very recent. A major reason has been the lack of an objective measurement system for what is widely assumed to be a subjective state. Some professionals have learned to live with this state of affairs and have focused instead on measuring the relation between treatment procedure and symptom change, while others have made do with approximate measures of relaxation. This chapter has argued that measuring relaxation enhances the assessment of treatment outcome. We have presented an objective method for measuring the motoric component of relaxation, along with evidence for its reliability and validity. This method is placed in the context of a multimodal conceptualization of relaxation. We regard it as a crucial but by no means complete metric. We hope it serves to stimulate further research on the assessment of relaxation and in the development of more effective training procedures.

Chapter Three

Behavioral Relaxation Training

This chapter presents the 'standard' Behavioral Relaxation Training (BRT) procedure for use with adults and older children who have normal learning capabilities. Training procedures for special populations are presented in chapter 4.

BEFORE TRAINING

BRT shares many elements in common with other relaxation methods. These include the setting in which training occurs, a general rationale for learning relaxation skills, and an expectation that the trainee will practice the skills. These common elements are discussed briefly below. The specific features of BRT are then presented in more detail.

The Setting

The physical and social environment should be conducive to relaxation. As discussed in chapter 1, in order for the trainee to observe the low-intensity events of interest, distracting and interrupting stimuli must be kept to a minimum. Lighting may be dimmed to provide a relaxing atmosphere, but it should be sufficient to allow observation of the trainee's behavior.

Full bodily support should be provided, so that the trainee need not exert effort to maintain his or her posture. A padded reclining chair with footrest is commonly employed, but care should be taken that the trainee fits the chair comfortably. Small pillows can be used to fill gaps that may occur beneath the trainee's elbows or lower back. If training or practice is done on a flat surface, pillows should be placed beneath the trainee's knees, forearms, and head, flexing the legs, arms, and spine slightly. This prevents discomfort from lordosis. We have found a beanbag chair to be useful for small children and this may also be acceptable for adults. Seating position for the trainer, to allow adequate observation of the trainee's behavior, has been discussed in chapter 2.

The Rationale for BRT

The rationale provides reasons why the trainee should follow the trainer's instructions. As described in chapter 1, these 'rules for relaxation' state the relationships between antecedents, behaviors, and consequences of relaxation. The specifics of this general formula are as varied as the individuals who are in need of relaxation training, and no universal prescription can be provided here. In general, however, the following steps are useful in developing and presenting a rationale: (a) Review the problematic behavior; (b) Present relaxation as an alternative; (c) Describe the training procedure.

First, the history and diagnosis process reveal that the trainee's current modes of responding are problematic. As discussed in chapter 5, problem behaviors occur in any and all of the taxonomic categories. Complex emotional, pain, and stress behaviors are costly and ineffective ways of responding to life's demands. A review of these costs and discomforts with the trainee enhances the potential reinforcing value of alternative behavior. In addition, there may be reinforcing consequences of the problematic behavior, such as attention from others, monetary compensation, medication, and release from responsibilities (Fordyce, 1976; Goldiamond, 1974). The benefits of relaxation and other aspects of the treatment program must outweigh these consequences. The history may also reveal the antecedents of the problematic behavior, the social and physical environments which increase the likelihood of problematic behavior. These antecedent events provide clues as to the situations in which relaxation will be most useful.

Next relaxation is proposed as a more effective alternative. Often a *structural* explanation is employed, in which relaxation is described as overriding the problematic condition. Such explanations are variations of Wolpe's incompatibility or 'reciprocal inhibition' hypothesis (Wolpe, 1958), in which relaxation is held to be antithetical to the problem state, be it 'anxiety', 'stress', 'arousal', 'distractibility', or whatever. A *functional* explanation can also be employed, in which relaxed behavior is presented as effective in gaining desired outcomes. For example, by relaxing the eyes, jaw, and shoulders, a headache patient may reduce tension and prevent pain. Or, by sitting quietly and observing slow, regular breathing, a hyperactive child may gain his teacher's approval.

Whatever the mechanism, the rationale emphasizes the positive consequences of engaging in relaxation. Since BRT is a new procedure without an extensive literature on treatment outcome, care should be taken not to imply a guaranteed benefit. No procedure has been found to be 100% effective (which is why new approaches are needed) and the trainer should make an 'educated guess' based on the literature on BRT and related techniques. Since progressive relaxation and EMG biofeedback both emphasize the motoric modality, it is reasonable to predict at least similar success for BRT.

Finally, the training procedure, along with expected time and practice commitments, is described. BRT is presented as a motor skill in which proficiency comes with practice. Although the relaxed postures themselves are usually learned very quickly, beneficial outcomes result from regular practice and from implementation throughout the day.

Organization of Training Sessions

A typical BRT session takes about a half hour, exclusive of acquisition training. Table 3.1 shows the recommended time intervals.

An initial adaptation period, in which the trainee is asked to sit quietly with eyes closed, allows him or her to 'shift gears' from the previous activities of the day to the task of learning relaxation. Adaptation is particularly important if EMG or autonomic measures are to be recorded.

Pre-training baseline observations, as described in chapter 2, allow the trainer to judge the trainee's progress over successive training sessions. The trainee relaxes all ten behaviors while the trainer scores the BRS and asks for a self-report at the conclusion of the period.

Acquisition time varies, of course, depending on the trainee. The duration of a proficiency training session may also be adjusted to meet the needs of the trainee. Some people, especially early in training, find it difficult to sit still for extended periods. This and other problems encountered in training are discussed in later sections.

Table 3.1. Outline of a Behavioral Relaxation Training Session (with approximate time requirements)

Procedure	Time Required
Adaptation	5–10 minutes
Pre-training Observation	5 minutes
Acquisition (First session only)	15–20 minutes
Proficiency Training	15–30 minutes
Post-training Observation	5 minutes

The post-training observation period provides a BRS score which, in comparison with the pre-training score, indicates progress in that session. It also provides a measure of relaxation over successive training sessions.

ACQUISITION TRAINING PROCEDURES

After presenting the rationale, answering questions, and gaining the cooperation of the trainee, the trainer is ready to commence. Initial acquisition involves four steps for each of the ten behaviors listed in the BRS. These steps are as follows:

1. *Labeling*. Each behavior is given a one-word label by which it can be conveniently identified (i.e. Hands, Feet, Body, Shoulders, Head, Mouth, Throat, Quiet, Breathing, Eyes).
2. *Description and Modeling*. The relaxed behavior is described and demonstrated by the trainer, as shown in Figures 2.1 through 2.9. Commonly occurring unrelaxed behaviors are also demonstrated.
3. *Imitation*. The trainee is asked to demonstrate the relaxed posture.
4. *Feedback*. The trainee is praised for correct imitation. If he or she does not display the proper posture, the trainer first provides *corrective instructions*. If after two or three such prompts the trainee is still unsuccessful, *manual guidance* is gently employed to move the trainee into the correct position. When success is achieved, positive feedback is given.

As each behavior is successfully imitated, the trainee is asked to maintain the posture or activity for 30 to 60 seconds and to observe the feelings that occur. He or she is also asked to maintain the trained behaviors as each new one is added. In this way, all ten behaviors are gradually built up. If the trainee should slip into an unrelaxed instance of a previously trained behavior, this should be gently pointed out and corrected. If the trainee should become 'stuck', unable to imitate or maintain a particular behavior after several prompts and manual guidance, the trainer should move on to the next item. The trainer should reassure the trainee that one does not expect perfection right away and that success comes with practice. Other problems that may arise are dealt with later in this chapter.

The sequence in which the relaxed behaviors are trained is left to the discretion of the trainer, but here are several considerations for developing a useful sequence of training. 'Eyes' should be left until last, since the trainee needs his or her eyes open to observe the demonstrations of the above behaviors. Begin with behaviors which pre-training baseline observations have revealed to be already relaxed, thus allowing the trainee to start on a successful note. Topographical grouping of behaviors according to body areas, rather than skipping from one part of the body to another, may facilitate relaxation in adjacent muscle groups and also aid recall by the trainee.

A Script for BRT Acquisition

The following is a suggested script for the initial acquisition session.

Hands

1. *Labeling.* There are ten relaxed postures or activities. The first relaxed posture is called Hands.

2. *Description & Modeling.* Your hands are relaxed when you rest them on the arms of the chair (or in your lap) with the fingers slightly curled into this claw-like position, like this [demonstrate as shown in Figure 2.7-A]. Your hands are not relaxed if the fingers are flat or curled into a ball [demonstrate as shown in Figure 2.7-B and C].

3. *Imitation.* Please show me relaxed hands.

4. *Feedback.* (a) Positive—That's good. Now just continue to relax for a few moments and notice how your hands and arms feel in this position. (b) Corrective—Not quite. Curl your fingers a little more so that a pencil could pass under your pinky. (c) Guidance—That's still not quite it. Here, let me show you. [Mold the trainee's hand into the desired posture.] After (b) or (c), go back to (a).

Feet

1. *Labeling.* The next posture is called Feet.

2. *Description & Demonstration.* Your feet are relaxed when both heels are resting on the footrest with the toes pointed away from each other, like this [demonstrate as shown in Figure 2.8-A]. Your feet are not relaxed if your toes are pointing straight up, turned outward too much, or if your ankles are crossed [demonstrate as shown in Figure 2.8-B, C, and D].

3. *Imitation.* Please show me relaxed feet.

4. *Feedback.* (a) Positive—That's right. Just continue to relax your feet and notice the feelings in your legs and feet as your do so. (b) Corrective— Your toes are still too upright. Just let your legs and feet flop apart. (c) Guidance—Allow me to position your feet properly. After (b) or (c), go back to (a).

Body

1. *Labeling.* The next relaxed area is called Body.

2. Description & Modeling. Your body is relaxed when your chest and hips are straight in the chair with no movement [demonstrate as shown in Figure 2.6-A]. Your body is unrelaxed if your torso is crooked, or any part of your back or hips are lifted from the chair, or if there is movement in your torso [demonstrate as shown in Figures 2.6-B].

3. Imitation. Please relax your body.

4. Feedback. (a) Positive—Good. Now take a few moments to notice the sensations as you relax your body. (b) Corrective—You seem to be a little twisted to your left. Rotate your chest slightly to the right while keeping your hips still. (c) Guidance—Manual guidance of an adult's torso is difficult, and social conventions regarding touching chest and hips should be considered.

Shoulders

1. Labeling. The next relaxed posture is termed Shoulders.

2. Description & Modeling. Your shoulders are relaxed when they are resting against the chair, and appear rounded, with the tops in a straight line [demonstrate as shown in Figure 2.5-A]. They are unrelaxed if they are raised or twisted, or if one is higher than the other [demonstrate as shown in Figures 2.5-B and C].

3. Imitation. All right, can you demonstrate relaxed shoulders?

4. Feedback. (a) Positive—That's right. Now just relax and observe the feelings in your shoulders. (b) Corrective—Your left shoulder appears a little higher than your right one. Lower your left shoulder a bit. (c) Guidance—Your shoulders still appear a little crooked. Let me place them in a straight position. After (b) or (c), finish with (a).

Head

1. Labeling. The next relaxed posture is termed Head.

2. Description & Modeling. Your head is relaxed when it is resting on the cushion, facing straight in mid-line [demonstrate as shown in Figure 2.1-A]. Your head is unrelaxed if it is tilted or turned to either side, or tilted up or down [demonstrate as shown in Figures 2.1-B, C, and D].

3. Imitation. Please relax your head.

4. Feedback. (a) Positive—Good. Now just take a few moments to notice the sensations in your neck as you relax your head. (b) Corrective—That's close, but your head is tilted a little to the right. Can you straighten it? (c) Guidance—Your head is still tilted slightly. Let me adjust it so it is straight. After (b) or (c) be sure to return to (a).

Mouth

   1. *Labeling.* The next relaxed posture is called Mouth.

   2. *Description & Modeling.* Your mouth is relaxed when your teeth are parted and your lips are open in the center, like this [demonstrate as shown in Figure 2.3-A]. Your mouth is unrelaxed if your lips are closed, or if you smile or lick your lips [demonstrate as shown in Figure 2.3-B and C].

   3. *Imitation.* OK, please show me how to relax your mouth.

   4. *Feedback.* (a) Positive—That's right. Now notice the feelings in your jaw and face as you relax your mouth. (b) Corrective—Drop your jaw and let your lips open a little wider. (c) Guidance—Manual guidance is not applicable.

Throat

   1. *Labeling.* The next relaxed area is termed Throat.

   2. *Description & Modeling.* Your throat is relaxed when it is quiet and smooth [demonstrate as shown in Figure 2.4]. It is unrelaxed if there is any movement such as muscle twitches or swallowing [demonstrate].

   3. *Imitation.* Please demonstrate a relaxed throat.

   4. *Feedback.* (a) Positive—That's good. Notice the feelings in your neck and throat as you relax for the next few moments. (b) Corrective—That's OK if you have to swallow occasionally, but then just go back to relaxing your throat. (c) Guidance—Manual guidance is not applicable.

Quiet

   1. *Labeling.* The next relaxed activity is called Quiet.

   2. *Description & Modeling.* You are quiet when you are not making any noise, such as talking, loud sighs, or snores [demonstrate sounds].

   3. *Imitation.* All right, please demonstrate quiet for the next few moments.

   4. *Feedback.* (a) Positive—Good. Notice the relaxed feelings in your throat and chest as you quietly relax. (b) Corrective—Please don't vocalize as you breathe out. (c) Guidance—Manual guidance is not applicable.

Breathing

   1. *Labeling.* The next relaxed activity is called Breathing.

   2. *Description & Modeling.* Your breathing is relaxed when it is slow and regular [demonstrate]. It is not relaxed if it is rapid, or if there are

interruptions such as coughing, yawning, sneezing, sniffing, vocalizations, or the like. [Note: The trainee is not told the specific number of breaths which serves as his or her criterion for relaxed breathing. In addition to the rate criterion, the trainer may wish to employ diaphragmatic breathing as described in a later section.]

3. *Imitation*. Please demonstrate relaxed breathing.

4. *Feedback*. Observe the breathing rate for at least one 30-second period and compare it to the baseline rate. (a) Positive—If the rate is less than baseline, say 'That's good, just continue to breathe slowly and regularly.' (b) Corrective—If the rate is equal to or greater than baseline rate, say 'Please slow your breathing.' (c) Guidance–'Please inhale slowly and deeply when I say 'in', and exhale slowly as I say 'out. 'Pace the trainee's breathing so it is slightly less than baseline rate.

Eyes

1. *Labeling*. The final relaxed area is called Eyes.

2. *Description & Modeling*. Your eyes are relaxed when the lids are closed as smooth [demonstrate as shown in Figure 2.2-A]. Your eyes are not relaxed when they are tightly shut, or if there is eye movement beneath the lids [demonstrate as shown in Figure 2.2-B].

3. *Imitation*. Please relax your eyes.

4. *Feedback*. (a) Positive—Good. Notice the relaxed feelings in your eyes and forehead as you relax for a few moments. (b) Corrective—Your eyelids are closed a little too tightly. Allow them to become smooth. (c) Guidance—Manual guidance is not applicable.

For most people, this initial acquisition procedure can be accomplished in approximately 15 minutes of the first training session. A brief review of the behaviors and their labels may be helpful at the beginning of the second session, but generally no subsequent reviews are necessary. (More elaborate acquisition training may be required for special populations, and this is described in chapter 4.) After acquisition, trainees move right into the proficiency procedure. Subsequent sessions begin with proficiency training.

PROFICIENCY TRAINING PROCEDURES

After all ten items have been learned in acquisition training, additional training is needed to reach criterion on the BRS and to promote relaxed behaviors in multiple response domains. Proficiency training involves instruction to the trainee, systematic observation of relaxed and unrelaxed behaviors, and verbal feedback to the trainee concerning his or her behavior. Suggestions to observe the feelings of relaxation are also a part of training.

Instructions

The trainee is asked to relax all ten areas. He or she is told to review the ten items and to observe the relaxed feelings in each area. He or she is told that the trainer will observe the relaxed and unrelaxed behavior and will periodically provide feedback. Here is an example of instructions which may be given to a trainee.

> For the next 20 minutes 1 would like you to relax all ten of the areas that we have covered. Just to review, could you give me the names of the ten areas? [Reinforce correct recitation, and provide corrective feedback for any omissions.] While you are relaxing, I would like you to silently review each of the ten areas and to pay attention to your posture and the sensations of each one. I will periodically observe your relaxation and if I notice any areas that appear unrelaxed I will say the names of those areas. For example, if I notice that your breathing is rapid or irregular, and that one shoulder is higher than the other, I will say 'Breathing [pause] Shoulders'. You should then pay special attention to the named areas and relax them more. Do not be concerned if you feel the need to move, like to scratch an itch or swallow. Just do what you have to, and then return to the relaxed position. For the last few minutes of the session, I will ask you to just continue relaxing on your own but I will not notify you of any unrelaxed areas. Do you have any questions? [Answer questions.] Fine, now please sit back in the chair and relax all ten parts of your body.

The Observation System

During proficiency training, the trainer systematically observes the trainee's behavior in order to provide feedback. A two-minute interval observation program is recommended. This is frequent enough to prevent faulty habits from developing but not so frequent as to be intrusive. This program is similar to the observational system for relaxation assessment described in chapter 2, but allows a minute to elapse between each observation interval.

Using the BRS Score Sheet, the trainer first counts the breathing rate for 30 seconds, and then observes the other nine items for 15 seconds. The trainer provides feedback by reporting aloud the one-word label for any item noted to be unrelaxed during the observation period. If all items are relaxed, the trainer should give positive feedback (see below). After one minute passes with no observation or feedback, the process is repeated. If a denser schedule of feedback is desired, observation and feedback can be provided every minute. Alternatively, a leaner schedule can be programmed by allowing more time to elapse between observation periods.

Feedback

The simplest feedback is to report the one-word label of any behavior observed to be unrelaxed. The trainee is instructed to attend to that particular area and relax it. If the label is not sufficient to prompt the trainee to correct an unrelaxed area, corrective feedback can be employed. As in the acquisition phase, corrective feedback is a brief description of what the client is to do in order to meet criterion for a particular behavior. Manual guidance is usually not employed during proficiency training. If a particular item is persistently unrelaxed, more acquisition training may be given prior to the next proficiency session.

If all ten items are relaxed, the trainer should provide positive feedback, such as 'Good, you are doing very well.' Some trainees respond better to positive feedback and it should be included with the corrective feedback, even though all ten items are not relaxed. For example, a trainee may be told 'Your breathing is nice and slow and even, but lower your left shoulder a bit.'

An additional feedback procedure, to be employed at the discretion of the trainer, involves showing the trainee his or her BRS score, from the post-training observation period, at the conclusion of the session. This score can be easily and quickly calculated. It can be presented as a numerical percentage, or it can be plotted on a graph to show progress over successive sessions. Care should be taken that this does not result in a competitive orientation by the trainee. Some might want to know how they compare to other trainees or become concerned about beating their previous score.

After the first proficiency session, the trainer should ask the trainee for his or her reaction to the feedback. Was it frequent enough or so frequent as to be intrusive? Was it helpful or was it seen as criticism? The primary criterion for effective feedback is behavior change. The percentage of relaxed behaviors should increase and be maintained at a high level in the post-training observation period. BRS scores of ninety percent or better, in the post-training observation period, are typically achieved within the first three training sessions. If this is not obtained, the trainer may want to reevaluate the feedback procedure.

Directing the Trainee's Observational Behavior

An important component of relaxation, as discussed in chapter 1, is observational behavior. Along with instructions for motoric (relaxed postures) and visceral (breathing) behavior, the trainer should provide instructions for the trainee's observational behavior. The trainee observes both overt and covert events. He or she observes (listens to) the trainer's voice providing feedback, and is mindful of his or her own postures. But whereas the trainer observes the trainee's behavior visually, the trainee observes the kinesthetic and proprioceptive events which occur as he or she relaxes. In this way, correspondence between public and private events is taught. The trainer may also direct attention to other private events, but has no independent means of verifying their occurrence.

A suggestion to observe one or two of the following events should be given every other minute, in alternation with relaxation feedback. First are the public events associated with the relaxed behaviors. Trainees can be asked to notice their smooth eyelids, open jaw, sloped shoulders, straight alignment of head and torso, curled fingers, and V-angle of their feet. Another set of events relates to feelings of heaviness in parts of the body and feelings of support provided by the chair. Trainees can be asked to observe the weight of their head, torso, arms, hands, and legs, resting against the chair. They can be asked to attend to the feelings of support where their head, shoulders, arms, buttocks, and legs come in contact with the chair. They can also be asked to observe the textural stimuli of the chair, such as the softness of the cushion beneath their head and the smoothness of the surface beneath their fingers.

The stimuli associated with breathing are also useful for directing observational behavior. Trainees can be instructed to notice how tension in the chest and shoulders increases slightly as they inhale, and how they relax as they exhale. The temperature differences between cool air as it is inhaled and warm air as it is exhaled can also be observed. Diaphragmatic breathing, if employed, provides additional aspects of breathing to be observed.

Concluding a Session

After 15 to 20 minutes of proficiency training, the trainer should say quietly, 'Just continue to relax on your own.' At this point, the BRS is scored for a five-minute observation period, as described in chapter 2, during which no feedback or other comments are provided. The BRS score may be quickly calculated and provided to the trainee at the end of the session.

At the conclusion of the observation period, the trainer should slowly arouse the trainee. He or she may say very quietly, 'Very slowly now I would like you to open your eyes.' A counting procedure is also useful. The trainer may say quietly, 'I am going to count to five; at the count of three please open your eyes, and at the count of five you may sit up very slowly.' A pause of one second should occur between each count.

When the client is alert, the trainer should inquire as to the events observed by the trainee. Which events were salient and which were not? Were any observations particularly calming and were any upsetting? (For example, one woman associated 'heaviness in the legs' with concerns about overweight.) In this way, an individualized list of relaxing observational behavior can be constructed for each trainee and used in subsequent sessions.

Summary

A proficiency training session comprises several elements. The trainer should first make sure the trainee understands the feedback system and answer any questions. The trainee is asked to relax the ten items that have been trained. The trainer systematically observes the behaviors listed on the BRS for a one-minute period and provides feedback at the end of each interval. Feedback may be in the form of the one-word label assigned to an unrelaxed behavior, a brief description of how to correct an unrelaxed behavior, or a positive statement noting the trainee's success. During alternate minutes, the trainer should direct the trainee's observational behavior to the sensations of relaxation, such as feelings of heaviness, support, calmness, and peace. After 15 to 20 minutes of training, a five-minute BRS scoring period is conducted, and then the trainee is slowly aroused. At the conclusion of a session, the trainer should inquire into the events observed by the trainee. A summary BRS score may also be provided to the trainee.

HOME PRACTICE

Relaxation requires practice if the trainee is to become proficient in the skill and reap the benefits of training. BRT is similar to other training procedures in this respect. There is consistent evidence that continued practice after the training regimen is an important factor in maintaining the long-term treatment effects (Blanchard & Andrasik, 1985; Reinking & Hutchings, 1981). The importance of home practice should be emphasized to the trainee.

The trainer should discuss with the trainee how to incorporate practice time into his or her daily routine. 'Homework' assignments and timemanagement counseling may be necessary to insure the arrangement of distraction-free time and setting which allows 20 minutes of practice each day. The considerations presented earlier in this chapter concerning the relaxation setting apply to the home as well as the office environment. As the trainee becomes more proficient, practice of mini-relaxation (see below) should take place throughout the day. Relaxation in an upright chair and diaphragmatic breathing (described in following sections) are also very portable relaxation procedures which can be done throughout the day. But these should not take the place of the daily relaxation period.

To help insure home practice and provide data on trainee progress, use of the Home Practice Form (Appendix D) is recommended. This provides a record of time practiced and self-reports of relaxed feelings. It also may help identify items which need additional training.

SOME PROBLEMS

On occasion, a problem may crop up in the course of training. Some are common to most relaxation training methods, while others are characteristic of BRT.

One class of problems, which has been reported in conjunction with both progressive relaxation training and meditation and which also may occur with BRT, has been termed 'relaxation-induced anxiety' (Heide & Borkovec, 1983; 1984). As an aside, the accuracy of this term in describing the phenomenon can be questioned. First, 'relaxation-induced' implies that trainees first engage in relaxed behavior and this in turn evokes unrelaxed behavior (Heide & Borkovec, 1984). Studies of the phenomenon have not shown any degree of relaxation; instead, they show that early in training some measure of arousal occurs, either self-report or physiological. Secondly, 'anxiety' implies a particular complex behavior which may not occur for all persons experiencing discomfort. A more generally descriptive term would be 'relaxation-training induced arousal'.

Arousal rather than relaxation may occur in any of the four behavior modalities. Examples include: *Motoric*—increased EMG in particular sites, restlessness, sudden 'startle' response; *Verbal*—self-report of discomfort, anxiety, or behavior in the other modalities; *Visceral*—shallow breathing, increased heart rate, nausea, vasoconstriction; *Observational*—vertigo, dizziness, attending to behavior in the other modalities.

How is the trainer to handle such reactions? No data have been reported on treating these phenomena, but several avenues warrant further investigation. Heide and Borkovec (1984) suggest that persons who fear loss of control, abandonment, or social evaluation are especially susceptible to adverse reactions to relaxation training. In such cases they recommended that further analysis and treatment be directed to these fears. Where such reactions are relatively mild and occur early in training, simple reassurance and encouragement to continue training may be sufficient. If the difficulty persists, increased attention to the particular response category may be helpful. For example, if the problem is vertigo, the trainee can be asked to concentrate observation on the spatial location of his or her hands and feet, or to open his eyes and fixate on an object in the environment. If the problem is muscle twitches, the trainee can be instructed in exercises to stretch (not constrict) the affected muscle group. Training can be shortened, either in duration or in the number of items covered, and gradually increased as the trainee progresses. Some people simply find it difficult to sit still for a lengthy period and require shaping.

A problem that sometimes occurs with BRT is that a trainee may not be able to exhibit a posture because of physical limitations such as unequal leg length, arthritis, scoliosis or other structural abnormalities. The trainer should be alert for such difficulties and make idiosyncratic adjustments in the relaxation criteria.

More commonly, a trainee may complain that a particular behavior is uncomfortable or does not 'feel right', due to a habitual tense or asymmetrical posture. In this case, the trainee should be assured that the discomfort is due to the newness or 'differentness' of the relaxed behavior, and with practice it will come to feel quite natural. We have observed that particularly with the Head, Shoulders, and Body, objectively symmetrical postures may initially feel 'out of line' to the trainee. For example, a person may be so accustomed to a slight turn of the head to the left that placing it in mid-line feels as though it were tilted to the right. With practice, such proprioceptive biases are corrected.

In some instances, a trainee may feel it is 'impossible' to perform a particular item and express frustration at the feedback that it remains unrelaxed. For example, they may feel unable to close their eyes without the lids twitching, or to breathe at a slower rate, or to swallow less frequently. They should be reassured that the trainer does not expect 100% perfection. Also, rather than negative feedback for unrelaxed behavior, the trainer can employ positive feedback for any instance in which the item does appear relaxed. Where difficulties persist, it may be helpful to combine BRT with other relaxation methods, as described in chapter 5.

VARIATIONS OF BEHAVIORAL RELAXATION TRAINING

BRT may be supplemented in various ways to promote generalization and to enhance its effects. These variations allow the trainee to engage in relaxed behaviors throughout the day in situations which do not allow the person to recline and totally relax. They are, in effect, partial relaxation procedures and are not to serve as substitutes for full practice. They help to strengthen the trainee's discrimination of arousing events and provide calming alternative responses for those situations.

Relaxation in an Upright Chair

An important aspect of relaxation is that it be portable. A central theme of this book is that relaxation is a skill which is usefully employed in a variety of arousing settings. Reclining chairs are not commonly available in most environments, nor is it possible to stretch out in full relaxed postures at work, at social gatherings, or while commuting. To enhance the generalization of relaxation to a wide variety of environments, a trainee may be taught to relax while seated in an upright chair. Such chairs are widely available—in offices, homes, waiting rooms, cars and buses— offering ubiquitous opportunities to relax. Such a skill is an integral part of the 'mini-relaxation' practice described below.

A study by J.D. Krmpotich (1986) measured tension levels of eight major muscle groups in six adults (three males and three females) as they assumed various postures while seated in an upright chair. From this and other research (Poppen, *et al.*, in press), we have devised an *Upright Relaxation Scale*, or URS, defining postures requiring the least muscle tension to sustain while seated in an upright position. After trainees have reached proficiency in relaxing while reclined, it is a simple matter to teach them the behaviors on the URS. The same procedures of modeling, prompting, and performance feedback employed in teaching the reclined behaviors are applicable in teaching the upright postures.

The Upright Relaxation Scale

1. Back

Relaxed. The spine is perpendicular to the floor, with the shoulder blades and the buttocks touching the back of the chair. A slight lordosis is desirable.

Unrelaxed. (a) Bent forward, so that shoulders are not in contact with chair back. (b) Leaning back, so that buttocks are not in contact with chair back. (c) Leaning to one side.

2. Head

Relaxed. The head is upright and motionless, with the nose in midline with the body.

Unrelaxed. The head is tilted forward or to one side.

3. Arms

Relaxed. Arms bent approximately 120° at the elbow with the wrists resting on the thigh, approximately half way between the hip and the knee. These dimensions may vary depending on the trainee's proportions.

Unrelaxed. (a) Arms akimbo. (b) Leaning forward on arms. (c) Arms hanging at sides. (d) Movement.

4. Legs

Relaxed. Legs straight and feet flat on the floor with approximately 90° angle at the knees and ankles.

Unrelaxed. (a) Legs crossed at knee or ankle. (b) Legs extended, so that knee angle is greater than 90°, or legs tucked under chair, so that knee angle is less than 90°. (c) Movement.

The following items are the same as defined on the BRS: *(5) Eyes, (6) Mouth, (7) Throat, (8) Hands, (9) Quiet, (10) Breathing.* Diaphragmatic breathing, described below, may be practiced while seated in an upright posture, using the hands as guides during initial stages of learning, in the same manner as described for practice in a reclined posture.

Mini-Relaxation

As the trainee becomes proficient in relaxing in the reclining chair, as evidenced by BRS scores, self-ratings, the Home Practice Form, and other measures, he or she can be introduced to the practice of 'mini-relaxation'. In essence, this involves relaxing parts of the body while engaged in other activities. It is similar in concept to Jacobson's (1938) 'differential relaxation'. Commonly occurring daily activities should be reviewed with the trainee to determine how and where he or she can employ mini-relaxation. Rehearsal and roleplaying of mini-relaxation in various situations can be incorporated into the training session.

Any of the behaviors defined on the BRS or the URS may be relaxed in the everyday environment, depending on the activity of the person. For example, the *Mouth* and *Throat* can be relaxed in non-social situations, where the trainee does not have to speak or be concerned with his or her mouth hanging open.

Breathing can be relaxed in situations not requiring speech or exertion. *Hands* can be relaxed in situations where they are not required for manipulation. *Shoulders* and *Back* should be relaxed while engaged in seated activities such as typing, driving or desk work. When a person is very actively engaged in a task, he or she should be encouraged to take periodic mini-relaxation breaks to literally 'catch his breath' by closing the eyes, breathing slowly and evenly, opening the jaw, lowering the shoulders, and curling the fingers. Such breaks may last from a few seconds to a few minutes in duration.

The trainer should point out that the trainee can use regularly occurring environmental events as reminders to engage in mini-relaxation. Such events as hanging up the telephone after a call, completing a section of a book or newspaper, or stopping at a red light while driving can serve as cues. For very busy people, a small dot of white typing correction fluid placed on the wrist watch face serves as a helpful prompt to take a mini-relaxation break.

Diaphragmatic Breathing

As discussed in chapter 1, breathing is a visceral behavior, the control of which is an important aspect of many relaxation training procedures. Rate and pattern of breathing, as well as a person's observation of his or her own breathing, are subject to instructional control. Thus a person may be instructed to breathe rapidly or slowly, deeply or shallowly, and to attend to his or her breathing.

One or more aspects of the following list of breathing maneuvers are characteristic of many relaxation and meditation training procedures (Bacon & Poppen, 1985):

1. Diaphragmatic breathing, in which the abdomen rises and falls while the upper chest remains relatively still.
2. Nasal breathing, in which air is inhaled and exhaled through the nose rather than the mouth.
3. Regular breathing, in which the rate and magnitude of inhale–exhale cycles is consistent over time.
4. Slow breathing, in which the rate is decreased from the non-relaxed state.
5. Observation of breathing, in which the person is instructed or instructs him or herself to concentrate on certain aspects of breathing.

BRT involves items 2 through 5 of this list, although only rate and gross disruptions, such as coughing, are objectively observed and scored.

Diaphragmatic breathing may have widespread effects on other visceral behavior, particularly vasomotor activity, though specific research on this issue is sparse (Bacon & Poppen, 1985). Diaphragmatic breathing may be useful for vascular-related disorders such as migraine, Raynaud's disease, and hypertension. It may also be helpful in disorders directly involving breathing, such as asthma and panic attack.

Training in diaphragmatic breathing should be begun only after proficiency has been achieved with BRT. Since trainees may achieve 90% or better relaxed behaviors on the BRS within as few as two sessions, diaphragmatic breathing may be incorporated into the BRT procedure very early.

The Rationale for Diaphragmatic Breathing. The trainee should be provided with a rationale for the additional training procedure. Diaphragmatic breathing can be presented as an enhancement of relaxation which has specific effects on the problem for which the trainee is seeking treatment. As stated above, the literature on the direct effects of diaphragmatic breathing is sparse, so the trainer should not overstate the case. A statement to the following effect creates a positive but not unrealistic expectancy.

Diaphragmatic breathing is based on methods that have been practiced for thousands of years for achieving calmness and reduction of tension. It involves learning to use the diaphragm, the band of muscle between the lungs and the stomach, rather than the shoulder and chest muscles, to draw air into the lungs. This allows more efficient breathing with less muscular work. It allows you to relax the neck and shoulder muscles while breathing. [This may be helpful for tension-related disorders such as headache and myofacial pain dysfunction.] Diaphragmatic breathing may result in relaxation in the vascular system. [This may be helpful for vascular-related disorders, such as migraine and hypertension.] It is incompatible with rapid, shallow breathing. [This may be helpful for panic attack, asthma, and stuttering.] And focusing one's attention on slow rhythmic breathing can have a general calming effect. [This may be helpful for anxiety disorders.]

Training Procedures for Diaphragmatic Breathing. Precise measurement of diaphragmatic and thoracic activity during breathing requires pneumographic or electronic strain-gauge equipment, which is beyond the means of most clinicians. Fortunately, it is possible for the trainee to place his or her hands so that both the trainee and the trainer can observe the relative motion of the chest and abdomen. The following procedure has been found to be consistent with measures provided by pneumographic recording (Bacon & Poppen, 1985).

While reclined in a relaxed posture, the trainee is instructed in the following steps:

1. *Hand placement.* Place your right hand on your stomach, between the bottom of your rib cage and your navel. [For most people, this is just above their belt line.] Place your left hand on your chest, on your breast bone (sternum) just below your collar bone (clavicle).
2. *Baseline breathing.* Now just breathe regularly, through your nose, and notice the rise and fall of your hands as you breathe in (inhale) and breathe out (exhale). [Observe the trainee and point out the occurrence of diaphragmatic or chest (thoracic) breathing.]
3. *Diaphragmatic practice.* As you breathe in (inhale), imagine your stomach to be a balloon which inflates, lifting your right hand. As you breathe out (exhale) the balloon deflates and your right hand falls. Your left hand remains still as your right hand rises and falls.
4. *Feedback.* Do not try to force it. Just attend to the motion of your hands and the feelings in your chest. Allow your right hand to rise and fall while your left hand remains still.

Some people find additional imagery to be helpful. Trainees can be instructed to imagine that their right hand is a boat, rising and falling on the slow, rolling waves of the ocean, while their left hand sits quietly at the dock.

The trainer should observe the motion of the trainee's hands for several breathing cycles. Some people are able to achieve the described pattern very quickly, while others have difficulty. Most are able to increase the amplitude of diaphragmatic breathing, as shown by the motion of the right hand, but continue to breathe thoracically as well. If this is the case, the trainer should comment approvingly on the diaphragmatic changes but should not strongly disapprove of the thoracic component, only mentioning keeping the left hand still. A shaping process should be employed, in which approval is given for one aspect of the breathing pattern, and, with practice, the other aspect declines. Some trainees may attempt to breathe deeply by raising and lowering their shoulders. The trainer should point this out and instruct the trainee to keep his or her shoulders still.

5. *Slow breathing.* Next, slow your breathing by pausing very briefly at the top and bottom of each breath. Just a half-second or so. Do not hold your breath or pause so you are uncomfortable.

6. *Additional practice and feedback.* The trainer should continue to praise positive aspects of the breathing pattern, with occasional corrective feedback for negative aspects.

7. *Tension release.* Notice how there is a slight increase in tension as you breathe in, and a decrease as you breathe out. Concentrate on the tension flowing out with each breath. A slight increase in tension as you inhale, and then let go as you exhale. Each time you exhale, feel the tension leaving your body.

8. *Combination with BRT.* Now we are going to practice the diaphragmatic breathing and the relaxed postures together. Silently review the relaxed postures to yourself, leaving your hands on your chest and abdomen. Also notice the motion of your hands, the slight pauses in your breathing, and the release of tension with each exhale. [Provide BRS feedback along with diaphragmatic feedback at two-minute intervals, as described earlier, for 10 to 15 minutes. By placing the hands in this fashion, the criteria for Hands and Shoulders on the BRS may be disrupted; this should be disregarded for feedback and BRS scoring.]

9. *Placement of hands at sides.* [After one or two sessions with the trainee's hands on the chest and abdomen.] This time, I would like you to place your hands on the arms of the chair (or in your lap). Continue to breathe diaphragmatically, with your abdomen rising and falling and your chest remaining still. Notice the sensations in your chest and abdomen as you breathe, and let go of all tension as you exhale. [There may be some disruption of diaphragmatic breathing when the hands no longer provide feedback, but this is usually transitory.]

Some Difficulties. Trainees often report some difficulty or discomfort when they first try diaphragmatic breathing. It is foreign to their usual breathing pattern, and the awareness of and attempt to control a behavior which is usually automatic can be disconcerting. These facts should be pointed out to those who express difficulty, reassuring them that their experience is not abnormal. Like any new skill, such as riding a bicycle or swimming, there is often an initial period of awareness of awkwardness. But by consistent practice, most people can learn to become proficient and comfortable with this new style of breathing. Reassurance, encouragement, and positive feedback are sufficient to deal with most problems.

In some cases, it may be helpful to take more time on each of the steps outlined above, rather than trying to accomplish them all in one or two sessions. Also, it may be helpful to provide additional BRT sessions before introducing diaphragmatic breathing. When making the transition from hands-on to hands-off, it is often helpful to allow the trainee to continue to use one hand, either on the chest or abdomen, in an alternating fashion, while placing the other at his or her side. The trainer should be careful not to blame the trainee for his or her difficulty and should take responsibility for the pace of training.

Conclusions

The variations described in this section have been applied in clinical settings by the author in a non-systematic fashion. That is to say, formal research has established only some of the more immediate physiologic results of these procedures (reduced muscle tension, increased hand temperature). They are consistent with the formulation of relaxation presented in this book, as well as with much clinical practice. But their clinical utility has not been demonstrated in controlled investigations and awaits further research.

Chapter Four

Behavioral Relaxation Training with Special Populations

The current emphasis on normalization and deinstitutionalization has accomplished much in teaching self-care and vocational skills to handicapped persons. It is apparent that such individuals also can benefit from relaxation training (Harvey, 1979; Luiselli, 1980; Ortega, 1978; Reiss, 1982). For example, surveys indicate that developmentally disabled persons suffer from a full range of emotional and behavioral problems, and may actually be more susceptible to emotional disturbances than 'normal' persons (Reiss, Levitan, & Szyszko, 1982). The disruption and demands caused by relocation from an institution to a community-living facility may be extremely stressful (Heller, 1982). Limitations in skills and opportunities may also be upsetting.

However, treatment of stress, pain, and emotional disorders of persons with developmental and other disabilities has received relatively little professional attention (Matson, 1985; Reiss, 1982; Reiss et al., 1982). Among the many factors responsible for this lack, the one relevant to this book concerns the limitations of the more common relaxation training techniques, particularly progressive relaxation and EMG biofeedback.

Progressive relaxation requires a large degree of verbal instructional control, which may pose a problem for trainees with limited verbal skills. At the opposite extreme, with biofeedback there is little that the trainer can specifically instruct the trainee to do to decrease the feedback signal. In contrast, BRT requires little verbal instructional control beyond 'Do this', accompanied by a modeled demonstration. An imitative learning repertoire is a very basic skill, which can be taught to even low-functioning individuals.

Both progressive relaxation and biofeedback emphasize discriminations of covert proprioceptive and kinesthetic events, which in 'normal' adults is accomplished through metaphor and reliance on an established repertoire of naming private events. With disabled persons, 'concrete' thinking and a limited repertoire make such discriminations especially difficult to establish. In this regard, we have observed that many 'special' people can easily do the tensing exercises of progressive relaxation training, but have difficulty with the release or relaxing part, ending up more tense than when they started. BRT emphasizes overt relaxed postures and actions which are easy for both trainee and trainer to discriminate. The 'problem of privacy', in which the trainer does not have access to the internal events of the trainee, is avoided. Because the relaxed behaviors are publicly observable (as is the biofeedback signal), immediate social or material consequences can be administered contingent on meeting specific criteria.

A related issue is the reliance on self-report as a dependent measure in progressive relaxation training. A handicapped trainee may be particularly influenced by the social contingencies controlling either compliant or non-compliant verbal behavior. The use of the BRS with BRT avoids this problem. (Of course the BRS can be used with progressive relaxation or any other procedure as a dependent measure of relaxation.)

An additional problem with biofeedback is that the wires and hook-up procedure may be particularly distracting and cumbersome for disabled individuals. The arousal generated by such devices may overshadow the relaxation task to be accomplished.

This chapter describes modifications of BRT which have been employed for moderately retarded and brain-injured adults and for hyperactive children. Trainers who work with 'lower-functioning' clients are encouraged to try these procedures. They are also urged to document carefully their observations and modifications of the procedure and, where possible, to publish their findings.

MODIFICATIONS OF BEHAVIORAL RELAXATION TRAINING

All relaxation training procedures are adjusted to meet the needs of individual trainees. Even the most 'standardized' procedures, such as Bernstein and Borkovec's (1973) version of progressive relaxation training, are modified for particular clinical or research protocols. Such a practice allows immediate gains, in that a particular individual or group may be better served. However, in the long run, unless the modifications are carefully documented, this practice adds nothing to our knowledge base of which procedures work best in which circumstances and for what reasons.

Each of the elements of BRT described in chapter 3 are subject to modification so as to better accommodate special populations. These elements include the setting, the rationale, the procedure itself, the use of consequences, and maintenance procedures.

Antecedents of Training

Setting. The setting for BRT with special trainees should follow the guidelines described in chapter 3 and elsewhere. Special care should be taken to make the training environment as distraction-free as possible, both with respect to intruding sounds from outside the room and visual stimuli within. It is a good idea to acclimate the trainee to the training room prior to commencing BRT, perhaps by using it as a place for review of various aspects of the trainee's program, or just for 'small talk'.

Organization of Training Sessions. Care should be taken that the scheduled training time does not interfere with some favored activity of the trainee. Initial sessions should be scheduled at least once a day, or more often if time permits. As acquisition occurs, sessions can be spaced out to three or two times weekly. The general training sequence outlined in Table 3.1 should be followed, but durations should be shorter, especially early in training.

Rationale. All trainees should be given an explanation for the training, according to their level of understanding. The purpose of training should be related to an area of benefit for the trainee, such as 'you can learn how to stop your headaches', or 'this can help you control your temper', or, simply, 'this can help you feel better'. Undue expectations should not be built up, but the idea of practice and improvement should be fostered. For example, a trainee may be told, 'relaxation won't make your headaches stop right away, but if you do this every day the headache's won't be so bad'. Trainees should not be summarily assigned to treatment but should be allowed to choose to participate or not and should be encouraged to ask questions.

Training Procedures

Acquisition Training. The same four steps described in chapter 3—of *Labeling, Modeling, Imitation,* and *Feedback*—are employed for each of the ten behaviors on the BRS. However, the entire process is slowed, with deliberate shaping of longer durations and chaining of successive behaviors. Extrinsic consequences may also be added to the social reinforcers. It is especially helpful to begin training with those behaviors which were already relaxed during baseline, so that the trainee may start off successfully.

The general strategy is to identify, label, and model the first item and request the trainee to imitate it for successive durations of 15, 30, and 60 seconds. The second behavior is trained in a similar fashion for 15, 30, and 60 seconds. The trainee is then asked to demonstrate both behaviors together for a 60-second period. A third behavior is then trained and imitated for 15, 30, and 60 seconds, and the trainee displays all three for 60 seconds. (In some cases, especially early in training for people who have difficulty even sitting still, we have found it helpful to count the seconds aloud.) This process continues until all ten items have been trained. Corrective verbal feedback is provided immediately, contingent upon any unrelaxed behavior occurring for a trained item. The trainee is allowed two seconds to self-correct, and then manual guidance is employed as appropriate. Praise is given upon successful completion of each temporal criterion.

Typically, one to three items may be trained in each session. Each session starts with the trainee being told the labels of all behaviors trained up to that point and being asked to demonstrate them all together for 60 seconds. Retraining of behaviors which do not meet criterion should be done prior to proceeding with new behaviors.

Token reinforcers, such as poker chips or pennies, may be useful for some trainees. Such a system can be part of an ongoing program in the training facility, or can be set up specially for BRT. The details of the program should be worked out with the trainee prior to training. Token delivery should be concurrent with praise for meeting a behavioral criterion. Tokens can be dropped into a jar or can, making a 'clink' sound, so that the trainee does not have to watch for token delivery. Tokens may also be taken away for disruptive behavior during the session. Tokens should be exchanged for back-up reinforcers immediately after the conclusion of the session.

Proficiency Training. After all ten behaviors are trained in the above fashion, the proficiency training procedure described in chapter 3 is employed, with a few modifications. The duration of the training session may be shortened to 10 or 15 minutes. Corrective feedback rather than the one-word label is often necessary, and manual guidance may continue to be employed. Positive feedback for relaxed behavior is effective for special populations, and should be interspersed during training. If a token system was employed during acquisition, it may be desirable to fade it out during the proficiency phase. If tokens are continued, they can be awarded at the end of the session on the basis of the BRS score obtained during the assessment period. Even without tokens, we have found graphic feedback, in the form of a histogram displaying the current BRS score along with previous scores, presented after each session along with suitable praise, is a good way to maintain interest and cooperation.

The proficiency criterion for special trainees may be set lower than for 'normal' people. We have used both 80% and 90% relaxed behavior on the BRS for two successive sessions, with a minimum of six training sessions. The capabilities of the individual trainee should be taken into account in setting a criterion, but the trainer should be careful not to underestimate these abilities and to be alert to ways to modify the program so as to improve success.

Maintenance Training. As with 'normal' trainees, special clients should be encouraged to practice on their own at times other than training sessions. In structured living facilities, practice time can be incorporated into their daily routine, with unobtrusive checks by professional staff. High-functioning individuals can make use of the Home Practice Form (Appendix D) to monitor their own practice and their progress. 'Mini-relaxation' training (Chapter 3) may also be appropriate for many people. The goal of BRT for 'special' trainees, as for any client, is for relaxation behavior to be incorporated into daily life.

BRT WITH ADULT SPECIAL POPULATIONS

The Developmentally Disabled

Bonne McGimpsey (1982) first demonstrated that developmentally disabled adults could be taught relaxation using BRT procedures. The primary goal was to develop and test the BRT modifications, described previously, and to determine the feasibility of applying them to members of this population.

Subjects. Two men and two women, ranging in age from 21 to 44 years, were referred for relaxation training by a rehabilitation evaluation and training center. While they did not suffer from a particular stress or anxiety disorder, their counselors judged that they could benefit from such training. Their WAIS full-scale IQs ranged from 67 to 79. They were fully ambulatory and none were on tranquilizing medication. Three of them attended a sheltered workshop for vocational training, which the fourth had previously attended. Two of the subjects were married to each other.

Procedure. Training occurred five days a week at a university office to which the trainees were transported from home or the workshop.

Sessions were 25 to 30 minutes in duration, including a five-minute adaptation, ten-minute training, and five-minute assessment periods. In addition to the BRS, frontalis and forearm flexor EMG levels and self-report of relaxation measures were obtained for each session. A multiple-baseline-across-behaviors design was employed (Hersen & Barlow, 1976), in which training was introduced sequentially across the ten items of the BRS. This was replicated in the four trainees. Baseline, post-training, and four-week followup sessions consisted of a ten-minute period during which trainees were asked to sit quietly and relax, but received no training, followed by a five-minute assessment period.

The training procedure was as described previously in this chapter, with the exception that the trainees imitated the relaxed behaviors for 15 and 30 seconds, omitting the 60-second step for new items. Rehearsal trials, in which the trainee demonstrated the current behavior plus all previously trained behaviors, did require a 60-second criterion. When all ten items had been trained, proficiency training continued until the trainee demonstrated 90% or better BRS scores for two consecutive sessions. No home practice or maintenance procedures were implemented. Reliability of BRS scoring was established with a trained observer behind a one-way window. Reliability ranged from 88% to 94% agreement between trainer and observer.

Results. The results of BRT on each BRS item for each trainee is shown in Figure 4.1. This figure shows the BRS scored in a negative direction, with decreases in unrelaxed behavior as a result of training. In general, behaviors unrelaxed prior to training showed rapid improvement with the onset of training. Inspection of Figure 4.1 indicates that some behaviors were consistently unrelaxed prior to training (e.g. Mouth, Feet) while others were consistently relaxed (e.g. Quiet, Body). Breathing presented the most difficulty, perhaps in part because it was the last item trained and received the fewest trials. All ten behaviors were trained within four to six sessions, with an additional two to five sessions necessary to reach the proficiency criterion of 90% (10% unrelaxed). There was some decrement in performance at the post-training and followup sessions, though not to baseline levels.

EMG levels during the assessment period, as shown in Figure 4.2, were not consistently related to BRS scores. Only trainee #3 showed overall low EMG levels in both frontalis and flexor throughout training, and even his frontalis increased to baseline levels at post-training and followup. Trainee #1 showed EMG increases at the start of training, with declining levels as training progressed; frontalis increased at post and followup sessions. Trainee #2 showed a marked increase on session 6, the first day of proficiency training, with a reduction to levels slightly below baseline thereafter. Trainee #4 had a marked increase in flexor tension at the

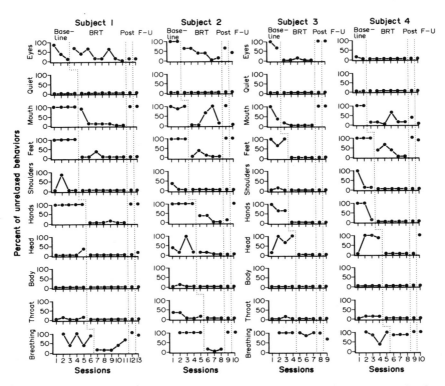

FIGURE 4.1. Percent unrelaxed behavior for each of the ten items in the BRS for four developmentally disabled persons. From 'Behavioral Relaxation and Assessment with Developmentally Disabled Adults,' by B. A. McGimpsey (1982). Unpublished Master of Science research report, Southern Illinois University—Carbondale.

beginning of training with a subsequent decline, while frontalis levels remained steady throughout training, with a subsequent decline by followup. The EMG increases at the beginning of a training phase may indicate the trainees' reaction to a new task. With practice, these levels usually declined.

Self-report measures for trainees #1 and #3 reflected their BRS and EMG scores, with improved feelings of relaxation as training progressed. Trainee #2's scores fluctuated throughout training, both higher and lower than baseline. Trainee #4 did not care for the procedure and reported feeling quite tense by the end of training.

Conclusions. This study demonstrated the feasibility of BRT with developmentally disabled adults. Such individuals learned the relaxed behaviors in a relatively few number of sessions. In some people, this learning is associated with reductions in EMG levels and improvements in self-

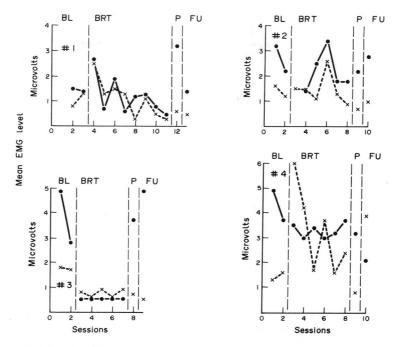

FIGURE 4.2. Mean frontalis (circles) and forearm (crosses) EMG levels for four developmentally disabled persons. From 'Behavioral Relaxation and Assessment with Developmentally Disabled Adults,' by B. A. McGimpsey (1982). Unpublished Master of Science research report, Southern Illinois University—Carbondale.

report. However, a number of limitations are apparent. The reasons for the individual differences in response to training are not obvious from this small n study. Another limitation was that the trainees were given no clearcut rationale for participating, other than that relaxation may help them feel better at work. Trainees who are motivated to alleviate some personally meaningful problem would be expected to show greater effects. Also, no maintenance procedures were employed, leading to decrements at followup.

The Brain-Injured

Individuals suffering closed-head injuries incur a variety of symptoms, including impulsivity, restlessness, and anxiety (Lishman, 1973). Such problems suggest that relaxation may be a useful part of treatment. Donna Zahara (1983) employed BRT with three young men in a residential treatment center for head-injured patients. In addition, Steve Taylor (1983) measured the effects of training on a variety of psychomotor tasks.

Subjects. The patients were referred for relaxation training by their clinical team supervisors who reported them to be 'nervous' or 'irritable', and who felt relaxation would benefit their motor control, social interactions, and general health. Trainee #1 was 22 years old and had been injured in an automobile accident three years earlier. He manifested both gross and fine motor skill impairments, such as in walking and writing. Trainee #2 was 30 years old and had been injured in an industrial accident over three years previously. He displayed impulsivity, restlessness, and social skill deficits. Trainee #3 was 29 years old and had been injured in a workplace explosion over one year previously. His problems included reasoning, memory, and speech impairments.

Procedure. Training took place in an office in the residential treatment facility. Sessions were scheduled three times weekly, and lasted approximately 30 minutes, including five minutes of adaptation, fifteen minutes of relaxation, and five minutes of assessment. Motor skills assessment took place after each session.

A multiple-probe-across-subjects design was employed (Horner & Baer, 1978). After training began for trainee #1, the second and third trainees were given baseline sessions whenever the first trainee met criterion for a set of three behaviors. When he met criterion for all ten items, trainee #2 commenced training. The third trainee remained in baseline, receiving measurement sessions whenever trainee #2 reached criterion for a set of three behaviors, and finally began training when trainee #2 reached criterion for all ten items. Baseline sessions were given to control for effects such as therapist contact and instructions to relax. The 'probe' format was used, rather than a strict multiple-baseline, to minimize the possibly aversive effects of repeated measurement in the absence of training (Cuvo, 1979).

The training procedure was similar to that described previously in this chapter. Training criterion was 80% relaxed behavior on the BRS in the five-minute assessment period, after which six additional proficiency training sessions were administered. Post-training and three-week follow-up assessments were then obtained. Reliability of BRS scoring was conducted by a trained observer in the training room, averaging 91% agreement. Frontalis EMG and self-report of relaxation were also assessed.

Two psychomotor tasks were assessed for all three trainees: a microcomputer game and the Placing and Turning tests of the Minnesota Rate of Manipulation Test (MRMT). Performance on the computer game and the MRMT were measured after alternate BRT sessions. Additional specific performance tasks were assessed for two trainees on alternate sessions. Trainee #1, who had difficulty writing and signing his name, was tested on a mark-making task while his forearm EMG was monitored.

Trainee #3, who had speaking problems, was tested for duration of breath control while vocalizing vowel sounds.

Results. Figure 4.3 shows that the trainees reached the 80% relaxation criterion in four to eight sessions, and maintained or improved this level in subsequent sessions. The BRS is scored in the negative direction, with decreasing scores reflecting increased relaxed behavior. Frontalis EMG levels showed no consistent change or relation to BRS scores. This may

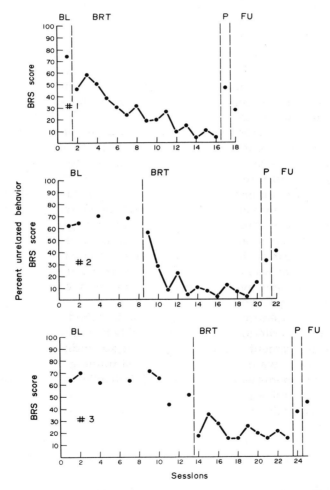

FIGURE 4.3. Behavioral Relaxation Scale scores for three brain injured men. BL = baseline; BRT = relaxation training; P = post-training; FU = followup. From 'Behavioral Relaxation Training with Traumatically Head-Injured Adults,' by D. Zahara (1983). Unpublished Master of Science research report, Southern Illinois University—Carbondale.

have been due to scar tissue and other damage related to the trainees' head injuries. Self-reports generally reflected an improvement in relaxed feelings during BRT.

No systematic change was observed on the computer game for any trainee, either in points scored or time to completion. Trainees #1 and #3 improved on the MRMT, but improvements during baseline for trainee #3 suggest this could have been a result of continued practice rather than BRT. Trainee #1 showed a large improvement in the mark-making task after BRT, accompanied by a decrease in forearm EMG. His therapist reported that he showed much improvement in his everyday writing. Trainee #3 showed no change in vowel production duration during baseline but demonstrated a steady increase in duration after BRT began.

Conclusions. As with the McGimpsey (1983) study, this project showed the feasibility of BRT with a special population. The training was included as part of each person's clinical regimen, to relieve general 'nervousness', with specific clinical targets for two of the trainees (handwriting and speech). Improvements in both these target areas were noted. Trainees were encouraged to relax on their own, but no systematic effort was made to incorporate such practice into their daily routine. Trainees were generally positive and cooperative about the relaxation training, but the repeated psychomotor testing was burdensome at times. Behaviors of interest and importance to the trainee are the most likely to show the benefits of relaxation.

HYPERACTIVE CHILDREN

Hyperactivity is conservatively estimated to occur in three to five percent of American school children, predominantly in boys (Barkley, 1981). Hyperactive children are characterized as impulsive, overactive, incapable of sustained attention, socially disruptive, and poor students. Stimulant medication, which has a 'paradoxical' calming effect in many children, is by far the most common treatment. Long-term drug use has raised serious objections because of growth retardation, somatic side effects, and lack of academic progress in medicated children (O'Leary, 1980; Werry & Sprague, 1974; Whalen & Henker, 1976).

Relaxation training has been seen as a possible behavioral alternative to drugs. As reviewed in Raymer and Poppen (1985), a number of studies have reported positive effects of frontalis EMG biofeedback or progressive relaxation on measures such as parent ratings scales, psychological tests, or academic and psychomotor tasks. Other research has found relaxation training to be no more effective than attention control procedures in improving performance. Many studies suffered from inadequate subject selection criteria, poor specification of procedures, confounded research designs, lack of followup, and inadequate measurement of training procedures and criteria. Another problem may be the difficulties inherent in learning the subjective discriminations required in EMG biofeedback or progressive relaxation training. As with handicapped adults, the objective nature of BRT should allow hyperactive children to easily learn the relevant behaviors.

BRT with Hyperactive Children

Rick Raymer contributed to the BRT modifications described previously by adapting the procedure for use with hyperactive children (Raymer & Poppen, 1985). This study showed the feasibility of applying BRT to members of this population and also demonstrated some benefits that may result from training.

Subjects. Three boys who had been referred to a community mental health center participated in this project. Trainee #1, 11 years, was referred by his family; trainee #2, 9 years, was referred by his physician; and trainee #3 was referred by his school. Trainee #1 was taking Ritalin 10 mg per day, which was discontinued during training. Parental and medical cooperation were solicited for all boys. All had been diagnosed as hyperactive by at least one physician, and also met the diagnostic criteria of Barkley (1981).

Procedure. Training was conducted in an office furnished with a large recliner and a one-way window. EMG monitoring equipment was first demonstrated to the boys, and then kept out of sight by draping with sheets. Reliability observations, for at least 25% of the sessions with each child, were made thrugh the one-way window by a trained observer in an adjacent room. Agreement between observer and trainer was better than 90% for each child.

Training sessions were conducted approximately twice a week. A multiple-probe-across-subjects design was employed, similar to that described previously with the head-injured men. Dependent measures included the BRS, frontalis EMG, parent ratings on the Hyperactivity Index of the Conners Questionnaire (Goyette, Conners, & Ulrich, 1978), and self-report, in which the boys were asked, 'Answer yes or no; do you feel relaxed?'

Training followed the format described earlier in this chapter, and employed token reinforcers in addition to praise. The tokens were spent after each session on an outing, treat, or trinket provided by the trainer.

After reaching criterion in acquisition, trainee #1 had difficulty meeting the proficiency criterion. At this point, during an outing, the trainer noticed that the child sat quietly in a beanbag chair. Reasoning that the beanbag provided better body support than the big recliner, one was employed in the next session, with an immediate improvement in relaxed behaviors. After the child reached the proficiency criterion, a reversal to the recliner was conducted, and then back to the beanbag. The same procedure was followed for trainees #2 and #3.

Parent Training. Followup measurements were conducted two to three months after training, and then the parents were offered the opportunity to learn the procedure in their home. All parents agreed to the program, including purchasing a beanbag chair and implementing token reinforcement. The trainer first conducted an initial home baseline session. Next, the mother was trained briefly in the relaxed behaviors herself, and observed the trainer conduct BRT and BRS scoring with her child. During the third and fourth sessions, the mother conducted BRT, following prompts provided by the trainer. Thereafter, the mother conducted BRT for ten consecutive days, with the trainer observing on the first, fifth and tenth day. A final followup measurement session was conducted in the home a month later.

Results. BRS scores for all three boys are shown in Figure 4.4. They displayed low or variable rates of relaxed behaviors in baseline, with no trend for improvement. Scores increased with the onset of training, but plateaus were reached between 40% and 70% relaxed. Introduction of the beanbag chair resulted in rapid achievement of the proficiency criterion (80% or better for two consecutive sessions) for all trainees. A reversal session in the recliner disrupted BRS scores, but they rapidly recovered when the beanbag was reinstated. Some decrement at one-month followup was noted, particularly for trainee #1, who was given a second session in which he was instructed to 'relax like you were taught,' resulting in immediate improvement.

Declines in BRS scores occurred for all three boys in the initial home baseline session. Performance immediately improved with training by the mother, and was maintained at the last followup.

Frontalis EMG data for each child showed a strong correspondence to the BRS scores, as shown in Figure 4.5. For trainees #1 and #2, there was a steady improvement during BRT in the recliner, with no large change when the beanbag was introduced. For trainee #3, EMG improved only slightly until the beanbag was implemented. Reversal effects are obvious for all three boys. EMG levels increased markedly during the home baseline session, but rapidly declined when mother implemented BRT, and were maintained at low levels at followup. Correlations between BRS scores and EMG levels were $-.42$ ($p < .05$) for trainee #1, $-.56$ ($p < .01$) for trainee #2, and -81 ($p < .001$) for trainee #3.

Parent ratings on the Conners Hyperactivity Index are shown in Figure 4.6. There was no systematic improvement during baseline. During BRT

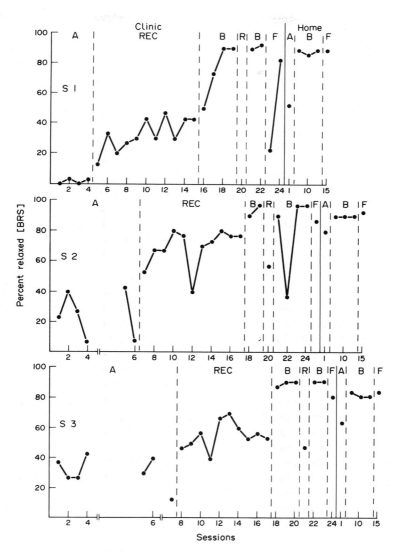

FIGURE 4.4. Behavioral Relaxation Scale Scores for three hyperactive boys. A = baseline; REC = training in the recliner; B = training in the beanbag; R = reversal to recliner; F = followup. From 'Behavioral Relaxation Training with Hyperactive Children,' by R. H. Raymer and R. Poppen (1985). *Journal of Behavior Therapy and Experimental Psychiatry, 16*, pp. 309–316. Copyright 1985 Pergamon Press, Inc. Used with permission.

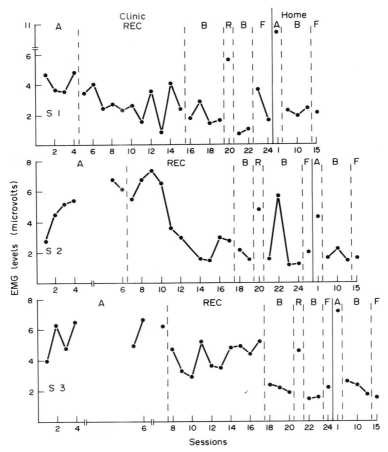

FIGURE 4.5. Mean frontalis EMG levels for three hyperactive boys. Phases are as designated in Figure 4.4. From 'Behavioral Relaxation Training with Hyperactive Children,' by
R. H. Raymer and R. Poppen (1985). *Journal of Behavior Therapy and Experimental Psychiatry,*
16, pp. 309–316. Copyright 1985 Pergamon Press, Inc. Used with permission.

there was a gradual improvement in ratings, with scores at the first
followup about one standard deviation lower than those at the end of
baseline. However, these scores were still within the 'hyperactive' range.
Scores for all three children markedly improved immediately upon home
training by the mother. They were all within the 'normal' range at the final
home followup.

   In addition to these formal measures, the parents were asked about
their reactions to the procedures. They all reported that it was convenient
and easily implemented and they felt it had benefited their children. They

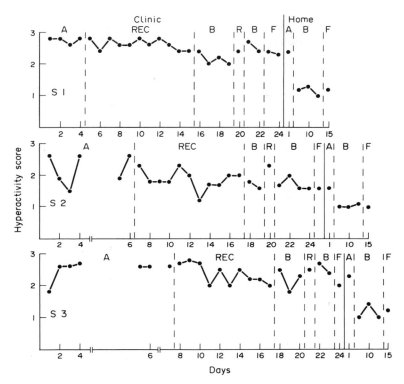

FIGURE 4.6. Parental ratings on the Hyperactivity Index. Phrases are as designated in Figure 4.4. From 'Behavioral Relaxation Training with Hyperactive Children', by R. H. Raymer and R. Poppen (1985). *Journal of Behavior Therapy and Experimental Psychiatry, 16*, pp. 309–316. Copyright 1985 Pergamon Press, Inc. Used with permission.

reported such things as a child employing the procedures on his own while watching TV or showing off his skill for relatives.

All children reported that they felt relaxed on every session, including baseline. This was taken as an indication that they were trying to please the trainer.

Conclusions. This project demonstrated that children meeting multiple diagnostic criteria for hyperactivity could learn to relax, as measured by the BRS and frontalis EMG. A beanbag chair proved to be an important factor, underscoring the need to provide full body support. Progress may have been quicker had a beanbag been provided from the beginning. Maintenance of relaxed behavior was generally very good, with decrements in performance easily remedied by instructions or brief training.

Effects of relaxation on the broader class of hyperactive behaviors were reflected in improvements on the Hyperactivity Index. Although no efforts were made to transfer the skills to the home environment during the office training phase, some improvements on the Conners were reported by all parents. When home practice was implemented, marked improvements on the Conners were noted. This may reflect actual changes in the children's comportment at home due to relaxation, or it may have altered the parents' perception of their children. Objective observation of child behavior would be needed to address this question.

Teaching BRT to Parents of Hyperactive Children

In the above study, the parents learned to administer BRT very easily, although at the time the children were already quite proficient in the relaxed behaviors. Ginny Donney (Donney, 1986) undertook to teach parents to conduct BRT in their own home right from the beginning. This avoided the issue of transferring training to the home environment, and demonstrated how easily a non-professional could learn to do BRT.

Subjects. The three boys in this project ranged in age from 8 to 10 years. They were all referred by their pediatrician, who judged them to be inadequately controlled by medication. Each was taking Ritalin daily at the start of the study. Medication was discontinued for trainees #1 and #3 prior to the last followup session, and for trainee #2 prior to the last baseline session. In addition to the medical diagnosis, the boys met the criteria described in Barkley (1981).

The parents were contacted by telephone and an interview was arranged in their homes to describe the program. All parents agreed to participate. Two purchased a beanbag chair and one was provided for the third because of poverty. The mothers of the first two boys and the father of the third participated in training.

Procedure. All training and observation was conducted in either the child's room or the living room, with efforts made to minimize distractions and interruptions. A simple AB design (baseline–training) with followup was employed, replicated across the three children, since time limitations prohibited the more elaborate multiple baseline. Training took place during the summer school vacation months. Sessions were scheduled twice weekly, depending on the commitments of trainer and parents. Each child's training program suffered one or more lengthy interruptions due to trips or illnesses.

Dependent measures included the BRS, frontalis EMG, and parent ratings on the Hyperactivity Index of the Conners Scale (Goyette *et al.*, 1978). The Home Situations Questionnaire (Barkley, 1981) was filled out by the parents, and the School Situations Questionnaire (Barkley, 1981) was filled out by the boy's teachers, prior to training and again at followup. Classroom observations were also conducted for trainee #2 on three behaviors ('out of seat,' 'talking-out,' 'on-task') by a teacher's assistant during baseline and by the trainer after treatment, since the assistant was no longer available. On 25% of the sessions, another trained observer accompanied the trainer to collect reliability measurements on the BRS.

Four baseline sessions were conducted with the trainer and parent both present. The child was asked to sit quietly for 20 minutes; the last five comprised the measurement period for scoring the BRS and recording EMG levels. After each baseline session, the trainer and parent discussed the BRS scoring. The parent was given a copy of the BRS definitions, and practiced the relaxed behaviors him or herself while the trainer provided feedback, guidance, and praise. Next, the trainer modeled relaxed and unrelaxed behaviors while the parent provided feedback.

Training sessions consisted of 5 minutes of adaptation, 20 minutes of BRT, and 5 minutes of assessment. The first three behaviors were taught by the trainer, with the parent observing and scoring during the assessment period. Training was conducted as described earlier in this chapter, including delivery of tokens for successful behavior. The trainer and parent reviewed their BRS score sheets after each session and corrective feedback was given for discrepancies. The next two behaviors were taught by the parent, guided by silent signals from the trainer. The trainer kept track of the observation schedule and indicated to the parent which behaviors were unrelaxed by pointing to her own body. The last five behaviors were taught by the parent, with the trainer providing corrective feedback after the session if needed.

After all ten items had been completed, proficiency training was conducted by the parent, to a criterion of two successive sessions of 80% relaxed behaviors during the assessment period. The trainer's role at this point was to conduct BRS and EMG assessments and to provide feedback and encouragement. Tokens were spent by the child as soon after the session as possible on small treats and outings delivered by the parents. Throughout training, the families were encouraged to practice on their own, though no systematic data were collected on independent practice. Two followup assessment sessions were conducted one and three months after the completion of training.

Results. Figure 4.7 shows the BRS scores for these children. There was no improvement during baseline for any trainee; if anything, performance worsened. When BRT was implemented, the children learned the ten items in five to seven sessions. Trainee #3 reached the proficiency criterion within four additional sessions, whereas trainee #1 required twelve more sessions. Agreement on BRS scores ranged between 90%

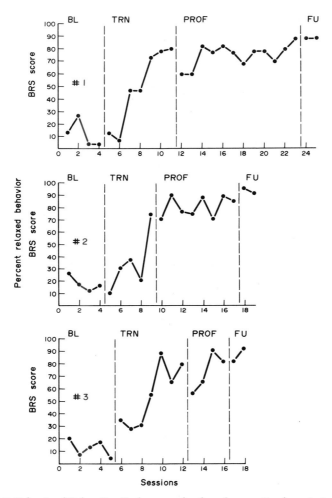

FIGURE 4.7. Behavioral Relaxation Scale scores for three hyperactive boys trained by their parents. BL = baseline; TRN = acquisition training; PROF =proficiency training; FU = followup. From 'Teaching Parents to Conduct Behavioral Relaxation Training with Their Hyperactive Children,' by V. K. Donney (1986). Unpublished Master of Science research report, Southern Illinois University—Carbondale.

and 93% for trainer and observer, and between 87% and 95% for trainer and parents, indicating that the parents became proficient scorers of the BRS.

Mean frontalis EMG levels during the assessment period are shown in Figure 4.8. Baseline values were generally high and variable for trainees #1 and #2, but showed a systematic decline for trainee #3. During BRT,

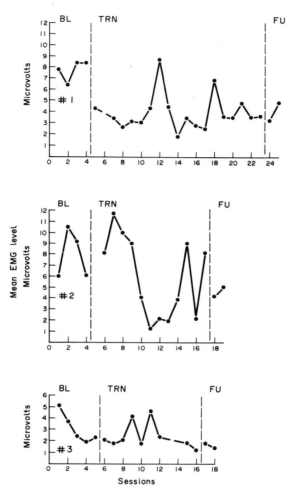

FIGURE 4.8. Mean frontalis EMG levels for three hyperactive boys trained by their parents. Phrases are as designated in Figure 4.7. From 'Teaching Parents to Conduct Behavioral Relaxation Training with Their Hyperactive Children,' by V. K. Donney (1986). Unpublished Master of Science research report, Southern Illinois University—Carbondale.

EMG values declined for all children and remained at low levels at followup. As in the Raymer study, EMG levels generally paralleled the BRS scores, decreasing as relaxed behavior increased. Correlations between these two measures were $-.72$ (p $<$ .001) for trainee #1 and $-.61$ (p $<$ .01) for trainee #3. The correlation for trainee #2 was not significant because of the unaccountably high EMG values in sessions 15 and 17.

Table 4.1. Parent ratings on the Hyperactivity Index and the Home Situations Questionnaire, and teacher ratings on the School Situations Questionnaire.*

Subject	Condition	Hyp. Index	HSQ		SSQ	
			Freq.	Rating	Freq.	Rating
1	Baseline	1.75	100%	5.2	63%	3.0
	Training	2.03	—	—	—	—
	Follow-up	1.15	50%	3.6	75%	2.0
2	Baseline	2.08	62%	6.5	75%	6.0
	Training	2.09	—	—	—	—
	Follow-up	1.90	40%	3.7	100%	7.0
3	Baseline	1.14	100%	3.7	66%	5.0
	Training	1.01	—	—	—	—
	Follow-up	1.00	50%	2.0	51%	2.5

*Adapted from 'Teaching Parents to Conduct Behavioral Relaxation Training with their Hyperactive Children,' by V. K. Donney (1986). Unpublished manuscript.

Mean parent ratings on the Hyperactivity Index of the Conners Questionnaire are shown in Table 4.1. All children evidenced an improvement (decrease in score) in the followup as compared to the baseline period. However, the changes during the BRT period differed. The scores for trainee #1 actually increased slightly during BRT, indicating worsening behavior, but at followup his scores declined to within the 'normal' range. Trainee #2 showed no change during training, with a small improvement by the followup period, but remained in the 'hyperactive' range. Trainee #3 had ratings in the 'normal' range during baseline, and showed an improvement during BRT which was maintained at followup.

Table 4.1 also presents the scores on the Home Situations Questionnaire (HSQ). For all children, the parents reported a marked improvement by followup, both in the percentage of situations reported as presenting a problem and in the severity rating of those situations. The School Situations Questionnaire (SSQ) was a different story. It should be pointed out that the teachers doing the post-training ratings were different than the ones doing the initial rating, since the children had gone to a higher grade, so there are many confounding variables in these ratings. Trainee #1 was rated as increasing in percent of problem situations, though the severity rating decreased. Trainee #3 was rated as improving in both percentage of situations and severity. Trainee #2 was rated as increasing in both percentage and severity. The child's teacher, upon learning he was 'hyperactive', tried to have him moved to a special classroom. In contrast, classroom observations indicated that the percentage of intervals he was observed to be 'talking-out' decreased from 23% to 8%, 'out-of-seat' decreased from 20% to 1%, and 'on-task' increased from 23% to 86%.

Conclusions. This study demonstrated that parents quickly and easily learned to conduct BRT with their hyperactive children, essentially conducting training on their own after the third session. The objective criteria for relaxed behavior allowed the parents to easily observe their children and reinforce their performance. The parents reported that they did not maintain a formal training program; however, the children maintained the relaxed behaviors at least two months after training, and the parents gave anecdotal reports that they spontaneously engaged in relaxation.

Some comparisons between this and the previous study are in order. First, there were no differences in the number of sessions required to reach a proficiency criterion on the BRS. It was felt that using a beanbag chair from the outset in the second study would speed up acquisition. Perhaps this advantage was offset by the fact that parents were conducting training, but it is more likely that reaching criterion was delayed by interruptions which occurred in the training regime, as the children took time off to visit Grandma or a divorced parent, or to recover from an illness or injury. Second, it was felt that conducting training in the home would facilitate general improvement in comportment, as measured by ratings on the Conners. Improvements on the Hyperactivity Index during training occurred only for trainee #3, who was a pretty good kid to start with. Improvements were noted for the other two, but only at followup. The lack of improvement during the training phase may reflect the fact that the children were home all day every day; improved parental ratings occurred only after the children were back in school. A third point is that none of the parents maintained training after the formal program was over, although they all felt it had done much good for their children. This points up the importance of training for maintenance, perhaps through a fading and followup program.

Chapter Five

Applications and Extrapolations

This chapter follows up the analysis provided in chapter 1, which described the similarities and differences of BRT and other relaxation training procedures. It was noted that BRT shares many features which make it effective in the treatment of disorders for which other forms of relaxation training are traditionally employed. The first section of this chapter presents two case studies which illustrate the use of BRT in the treatment of a phobic disorder, for which progressive relaxation training is commonly used, and in the treatment of migraine headache, for which thermal biofeedback training is often employed. These cases provide the practitioner with the details of a treatment program incorporating BRT, as well as information on problems which often crop up in clinical practice and possible solutions.

The second section of this chapter provides a more general analysis of the classes of problems for which relaxation is prescribed, employing the same taxonomy of behavior used in the analysis of relaxation. This analysis provides a rationale for the effectiveness of relaxation and for selecting among the various training procedures.

CASE STUDIES OF BRT IN CLINICAL PRACTICE

BRT in the Systematic Desensitization of a Phobia

Systematic desensitization has a long history in the treatment of phobia, representing one of the first behavioral techniques for the treatment of adult anxiety disorders (Wolpe, 1958). This procedure involves training the phobic client in relaxation; traditionally, progressive muscle relaxation training has been used for this. A hierarchy is constructed, consisting of a list of stimulus situations, arranged from least to most aversive, associated with the phobic behavior. Then, while the client is deeply relaxed, the therapist verbally describes an item on the hierarchy which the client vividly imagines. If the client remains calm while imagining this scene, a slightly more aversive item on the list is presented next. In this way, the client works his or her way through the hierarchy. He or she is also encouraged to try out successfully completed items in real life.

In his original formulation, Wolpe proposed that the autonomic state of relaxation 'reciprocally inhibited' the autonomic state of anxiety. By relaxing in the presence of cues which ordinarily elicit anxious arousal, the connection between those stimuli and anxiety responses are broken. In the formulation presented later in this chapter, it is proposed that anxious behaviors occur in all modalities and not just the visceral one. Incompatible behaviors in the various modalities, generated by relaxation as well as other aspects of systematic desensitization, serve to counteract anxious behavior. The general principle is the same, however; anxious responses to certain situations are replaced by incompatible adaptive behaviors.

Sharonlynne Helfer (1984) undertook the treatment of a phobic client, using BRT in an otherwise standard systematic desensitization framework. Special efforts were made to assess behavior in the various modalities throughout the course of treatment in order to determine the factors responsible for outcome.

The Client. Mr. A was a 30-year-old white male, married, with two children, a high-school graduate employed in a blue-collar profession. He was referred to the university clinical center by his physician for a longstanding fear of crossing bridges.

Assessment and Hierarchy Construction. Social history and specific information concerning his fears were obtained in unstructured interviews as well as from the Fear Questionnaire (Marks & Mathews, 1979) and the Fear Survey Schedule (Wolpe & Lang, 1964). In addition, Mr. A was instructed to self-record instances of fearsome situations as he went about his daily affairs. This information was discussed in subsequent interviews.

Mr. A reported having had a fear of crossing bridges since childhood and could recall no precipitating event. In addition, he reported fears of his own blood and of heights. The bridge phobia interfered with his social and family life, in that he avoided making automobile trips which necessitated crossing bridges. In those instances in which he had confronted a bridge, he reported having to have his wife or friend drive; he closed his eyes during the crossing and experienced trembling, sweating, rhinorrhea, difficulty concentrating, and embarrassment that his children or friends could see his reactions. He negotiated small highway overpasses in the course of driving to work without difficulty.

Mr. A was given a rationale for systematic desensitization emphasizing the incompatibility between relaxation and anxiety. By relaxing in the presence of imaginal cues associated with anxiety, he was told that he would learn to remain calm when confronted with similar situations outside the training room.

A 19-item hierarchy was constructed, involving the dimensions of: people present in the car, who is driving, particular bridges, time before a trip, proximity to or location on a bridge, day or night. These were rated by Mr. A on a 100-point Subjective Unit of Disturbance Scale (Wolpe & Lazarus, 1966) and constructed so there was a smooth progression from low to high items. In addition, three maximum intensity items were employed as *probe* stimuli, which were inserted at various points throughout the desensitization program, to determine the client's reaction to scenes presented out of sequence.

Dependent measures in the motoric, visceral, and verbal modalities were assessed. Observational behavior was only assessed informally by asking the client how clearly he could imagine the hierarchy items. Motoric measures consisted of the BRS and trapezius EMG levels. The visceral measure consisted of heart rate (HR). The verbal measure consisted of self-report on the tension/relaxation scale (Appendix C). Motoric and visceral measures were taken during the course of each training and desensitization session as well as during a five-minute post-training observation period. The verbal measure was collected at the end of the observation period. Two baseline sessions preceded training, consisting of five minutes adaptation, 20 minutes of relaxing with no specific instructions, and five minutes of observation.

Behavioral Relaxation Training. BRT began after the start of hierarchy construction and the baseline observations. We had anticipated that an advantage of BRT was that the relaxed behaviors could be learned quickly. Although Mr. A's scores on the BRS showed rapid acquisition, as shown in Figure 5.1, his responses in other modalities indicated that a generalized response class of relaxed behaviors developed more slowly.

Specifically, Mr. A reported extreme discomfort in the first BRT session, as shown in Figure 5.2. While this could be interpreted as 'relaxation induced anxiety', we sought to determine what features of training were aversive. Mr. A reported concern about being watched and evaluated. He experienced difficulty relaxing his eyes, for example, and felt that negative feedback increased the pressure on him to perform. Reassurance and continued practice decreased his reported discomfort somewhat. A

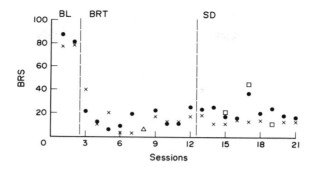

FIGURE 5.1. Percent unrelaxed behavior, as measured on the Behavioral Relaxation Scale, for Mr. A. Phases: BL = baseline; BRT = Behavioral Relaxation Training; SD = systematic desensitization. Legend: ● = post-training observation; × = mean during training; △ = identical value for training and post-training; □ = probe items. From 'Systematic Desensitization with Behavioral Relaxation Training: Assessment of Cognitive, Physiological, and Behavioral Response Systems,' by S. Helfer (1984). Unpublished Master of Science research report, Southern Illinois University—Carbondale.

change was made to positive feedback in the fourth BRT session and his self-reports of relaxation improved over the next six training sessions, as shown in Figure 5.2. However, without direct feedback on unrelaxed behaviors, his BRS performance worsened slightly, from 6% unrelaxed in the post-training observation period on the third BRT session to 25% unrelaxed on the final training session (see Figure 5.1).

Trapezius EMG levels were not directly related to BRS or to self-report scores during training. Figure 5.3 shows that there was an increase in tension in the first BRT session which subsequently declined. Tension levels increased again later in training, but decreased on the final session. EMG levels during training and in the post-training observation period were highly similar.

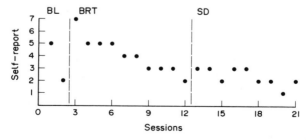

FIGURE 5.2. Tension/Relaxation Scale scores for Mr. A. Phases are as designated in Fig. 5.1. From 'Systematic Desensitization with Behavioral Relaxation Training: Assessment of Cognitive, Physiological, and Behavioral Response Systems,' by S. Helfer (1984). Unpublished Master of Science research report, Southern Illinois Univeristy—Carbondale.

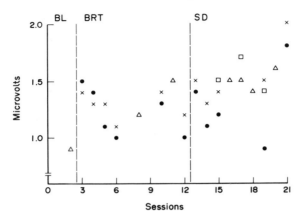

FIGURE 5.3. Trapezius EMG levels for Mr. A. Some scores are missing due to equipment failure. Phases and Legend are as designated in Fig. 5.1. From 'Systematic Desensitization with Behavioral Relaxation Training: Assessment of Cognitive, Physiological, and Behavioral Response Systems,' by S. Helfer (1984). Unpublished Master of Science research report, Southern Illinois University—Carbondale.

Relaxation training-induced arousal is also indicated by the HR measure. Figure 5.4 shows that HR increased in the second training session but subsequently declined to rates below those in baseline. HR measures during training were slightly but consistently higher than during the post-training observation period.

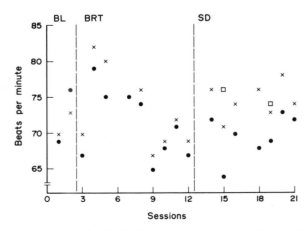

FIGURE 5.4. Heart rate scores for Mr. A. Some scores are missing due to equipment failure. Phases and Legend are as designated in Fig. 5.1. From 'Systematic Desensitization with Behavioral Relaxation Training: Assessment of Cognitive, Physiological, and Behavioral Response Systems,' by S. Helfer (1984). Unpublished Master of Science research report, Southern Illinois University—Carbondale.

Systematic Desensitization. In each systematic desensitization session, Mr. A was first asked to engage in the relaxed postures for 10 minutes. He did not receive specific negative feedback for unrelaxed postures during this time, but was given generally encouraging positive statements. He was then instructed to vividly imagine a scene read by the therapist, being careful not to add other elements to the scene. He was asked to signal by raising his index finger when he had a clear image of the scene, and to use the same signal if he became anxious while imagining it. Mr. A never signalled that he felt anxious. He was told that, on a few occasions, a high-ranking item (90 to 100 SUDS) would be presented before reaching the top of the hierarchy.

Each item was presented three times for successive durations of 15, 30, and 45 seconds, with approximately 30 to 60 seconds between presentations. Immediately after the therapist read the item she scored the BRS (with the exception of Breathing because of the short time involved); HR was sampled at five-second intervals, and mean EMG levels were automatically recorded. If Mr. A exhibited unusual unrelaxed behavior while imagining a scene, the therapist provided appropriate relaxation instructions before presenting the next scene.

Each session (after the first) started with one 45-second presentation of the last scene successfully imagined in the previous session. In the middle of the third, fifth, and seventh desensitization sessions (Sessions 15, 17, and 19), 90 or 100-SUD probe items were presented for 45 seconds.

Desensitization proceeded very smoothly for Mr. A. As stated previously, he never signalled that he felt anxious, even when the probe items were presented. His BRS scores were generally consistent with his (lack of) report. Figure 5.1 shows his BRS scores averaged for all scene presentations in each session. He generally displayed only one (out of nine) unrelaxed behavior — usually Eyes. In fact, BRS scores while imagining scenes were better than during the corresponding post-training observation periods. BRS scores were consistent for successive presentations of the same item. Mr. A displayed increased unrelaxed behavior during the presentation of the first probe item (Session 15), and a marked increase during the presentation of the second probe item (Session 17); however, there was no increase during the third probe item (Session 19).

Post-training self-report, as shown in Figure 5.2, was always in the 'relaxed' part of the scale. It showed an improvement over successive desensitization sessions, with a maximum level of relaxation reported after the penultimate session.

EMG levels during desensitization were slightly higher than during initial relaxation training, as shown in Figure 5.3. As with BRS scores, levels during the first two probe items were elevated, but the level during the last probe showed little change. Mean EMG levels during scene presentations were equal to or slightly higher than during post-training observation. Figure 5.3 indicates there was an increase in the final two desensitization sessions when the higher ranked items were presented. What is not shown is that EMG levels consistently declined over the successive presentations of the last two items on the hierarchy.

Figure 5.4 shows that heart rate, like EMG levels, was slightly higher during the desensitization sessions than during relaxation training. Like the BRS and EMG, HR was elevated during the first probe item but not during the final probe; unfortunately, equipment failure prevented a reading during the second probe item. A consistent finding was that HR declined over the successive presentations of each item; HR also generally declined over successive items within each session. Like the BRS, HR was lower during the post-sessions observation than during item presentations.

In Vivo Assessment. After completion of the hierarchy, Mr. A accompanied the therapist on two automobile trips over two large river bridges, each located about 60 miles from the university. The therapist drove, with Mr. A in the passenger seat and a technician in the rear seat who monitored HR equipment. HR was recorded at approximately 5-second intervals once the bridge was in sight. Each session consisted of two bridge crossings over and back.

During each trip, Mr. A was alert and smiling, looking around and commenting on how easy it was. No instances of hiding his eyes, trembling, sweating, or wiping his nose were observed. HR was variable with often high readings, which may have been due to movement artifacts. Highest rates occurred at first sight of the bridge, with a decline while crossing, and a further decline after the crossing was complete.

Followup. Approximately three months after completion of the last *in vivo* assessment, Mr. A again filled out the questionnaires and reported on his bridge crossing activities in an interview. His fear of bridges on the Fear Questionnaire declined to a rating of 1; his blood/injury score also declined to 1. On the Fear Survey Schedule, there was a slight increase in items related to blood and injury and no change with regard to heights. Mr. A reported that he had made several bridge crossings, both as driver and passenger, with no ill effects. He expressed great pleasure at his expanded social and family activities, such as going to major league ball games and big-city restaurants.

Discussion. What are the variables responsible for this positive clinical outcome? Specifically, what did BRT contribute to the treatment package?

At first it appeared that BRT was counterproductive, with the client reporting discomfort and manifesting elevated EMG and HR, despite engaging in relaxed behavior as defined by the BRS. Such dysynchrony points up the separability of the components of the response class called 'relaxation' and the importance of multimodal assessment. This initial arousal may have contributed to the therapeutic outcome, in that Mr. A learned firsthand that he could overcome anxious feelings, just as agoraphobic patients learn that their arousal is not fatal. The therapists also learned a lesson—about the reactive effects of observation and the importance of adjusting the training procedure to meet the needs of individual clients, as discussed in chapters 2 and 3.

With continued BRT, a fair degree of concurrence between response modalities was achieved. When desensitization was implemented, some concurrence and some differential responding was obvious. According to self-report (finger raising), Mr. A felt calm throughout all item presentations. But the BRS, EMG, and HR measures indicated arousal during the presentation of the first two probe items. Perhaps such arousal was not sufficient to be observed or labeled as 'anxiety' by Mr. A. The effectiveness of the BRS in detecting unreported arousal may be useful to the clinician who does not have access to electronic monitoring equipment.

Overall, Mr. A learned to remain calm, in motoric, verbal, and visceral modalities, while imagining himself engaging in formerly fearsome behavior. How did this translate into actual practice? As discussed in a later section, one means is through a change in 'rules', verbal statements about one's behavior and its consequences. This was shown in Mr. A's eagerness to put his skills to the test in the *in vivo* assessment trips. His success on these excursions strongly reinforced his changed behaviors, and led to continued success.

BRT with Migraine Headache

Relaxation training has been extensively employed in the treatment of migraine headache by Blanchard and his associates (Blanchard & Andrasik, 1985). Studies summarized by these authors concluded that a package involving eight weeks of progressive relaxation training with imagery instruction resulted in approximately 26% of migraine and migraine + tension patients attaining a success criterion for headache reduction. (The headache measure and success criterion is described below). Because of this relatively meager showing, the treatment package was expanded to include an additional 12 to 16 sessions of finger temperature biofeedback, along with autogenic phrases and imagery instruction. Successful outcome with the expanded package was effectively doubled over relaxation alone (Blanchard & Andrasik, 1985).

The rationale for employing relaxation in the treatment of headache has generally followed the stress model. This is a largely physiologic model, focusing on visceral responses to a variety of life events. Specifically, migraine sufferers are thought to respond to stressful events with intercerebral vasoconstriction, followed by rebound vasodilation which produces great pain (Olton & Noonberg, 1980). Relaxation, according to this model, serves as a prophylactic, preventing or reversing the initial vasoconstrictive reaction. A broader view of the effects of relaxation, in motoric, verbal, and observational modalities, in addition to the visceral modality, is presented later in this chapter.

The Client. Miss B was a 34-year-old white, unmarried woman, with a ten-year history of headache. She was a college graduate, employed in a managerial position. She referred herself for treatment to the Stress Disorders Clinic, a treatment research facility well known in the area.

Assessment. Miss B received the intensive assessment battery employed by the Stress Disorders Clinic (details may be found in Blanchard & Andrasik, 1985). This included a structured interview on headache history and psychological functioning, physiological measurement under rest and stress conditions, and a computerized psychological test battery.

Miss B met the criteria for migraine as described by Blanchard and Andrasik (1985). Specifically, she reported that she experienced intense, throbbing pain in the right temple region, accompanied by nausea and sometimes vomiting, sensitivity to light, sounds, and odors, with an episode lasting about 24 hours. She reported occasional prodromes in form of a feeling of pressure in her head, and in the past had experienced visual prodromes. Currently most of her headaches were nocturnal in onset and thus she had no awareness of preceding sensations. She reported about half her headaches were associated with menstruation. Alcohol, especially red wine, and certain foods were also associated with headache occurrence. She had been diagnosed by a neurologist as 'classic migraine'.

In addition, Miss B carried a diagnosis of bipolar depressive disorder, of six years duration, which was controlled by lithium. She reported few current depressive symptoms. Her Beck Depression Inventory score was 11 before training, and 10 at followup.

The principal measuring instrument was the Headache Diary, a sheet of paper on which, four times daily, she rated her headache on a six-point scale (e.g., 0 = no headache; 3 = moderate headache, pain is noticeably present; 5 = extremely intense headache, incapacitated). A weekly Headache Index was computed by summing all scores and dividing by seven, thus incorporating both frequency and intensity into a single measure. She also noted all medications taken for headache. Medication intake was the weekly sum of all medications scored according to a seven-point potency scale (e.g., aspirin = 1; codeine = 4; morphine = 7). Miss B kept her Headache Diary for a four-week baseline period, four weeks during the course of treatment, four weeks following treatment, and for a six-week period six months after completing treatment.

During each treatment session, frontalis EMG, cervical trapezius EMG, finger temperature, and the BRS were measured in a five-minute pre- and post-training observation period. Self-report of relaxation was measured after each observation period on the seven-point scale (Appendix C).

Treatment. Miss B was given the stress rationale, described above, and was told that relaxation would provide her with a means by which she could control her arousal and particularly her vascular reactions. A three-phase treatment program was outlined, each phase to consist of six sessions over a four-week period, with four weeks between each phase to assess its effects before going on to the next one. The first phase was to consist of Behavioral Relaxation Training, the second phase of digital temperature biofeedback, and the third phase of stress identification and problem-solving. As it turned out, headache frequency was reduced to such an extent after the first phase that the other two were not implemented.

Regular BRT was carried out as described in chapter 3, for the first two sessions. In the third and fourth sessions, diaphragmatic breathing training was added to BRT. In the fifth and sixth sessions, Upright Relaxation Training, along with diaphragmatic breathing, was implemented. These variations of BRT are also described in chapter 3. Homework practice of these procedures was encouraged and discussed in the treatment sessions. The use of diaphragmatic breathing and 'mini-relaxation' throughout the day was emphasized as an immediate tool to counteract arousal and maintain calmness.

Miss B learned the relaxed behaviors very rapidly. Her BRS scores, shown in Figure 5.5, and her self-report scores, shown in Figure 5.6, were

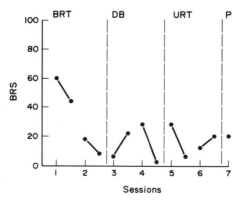

FIGURE 5.5. Percent unrelaxed behavior, as measured on the Behavioral Relaxation Scale, for Miss B. Phases: BRT = Behavioral Relaxation Training; DB = diaphragmatic breathing; URT = Upright Relaxation Training; P = post-treatment assessment. Legend: Each pair of scores connected by a line indicates the pre- and post-training measure for that session.

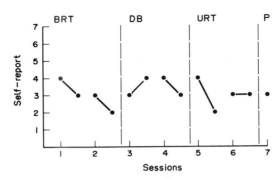

FIGURE 5.6. Tension/Relaxation Scale scores for Miss. B. Phases and Legend are as designated in Fig. 5.5.

closely parallel (Pearson r = .59, p < .05). She reached 8% unrelaxed by the end of the second session and reported herself to be 'deeply and completely relaxed'. Introduction of diaphragmatic breathing in session three resulted in an increase in unrelaxed behavior and self-report, but by the end of session four, scores were again low. Both BRS and self-report scores were elevated at the start of Upright Relaxation Training (session 5), as would be expected, but decreased with training. Relaxed behavior (while reclined) was maintained at session seven, an assessment session after completion of the post-training period.

Frontalis EMG levels during training are shown in Figure 5.7, and cervical EMG levels are shown in Figure 5.8. Variability in these measures, and fluctuations due to upright training, resulted in no significant correlation between these measures with each other or with any other measure.

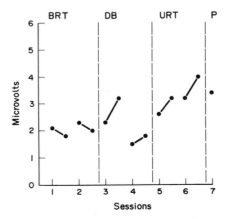

FIGURE 5.7. Frontalis EMG levels for Miss B. Phases and Legend are as designated in Fig. 5.5.

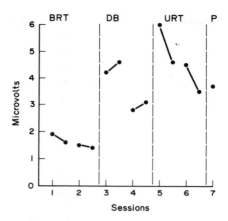

FIGURE 5.8. Cervical trapezius EMG levels for Miss. B. Phases and Legend are as designated in Fig. 5.5.

Values in both areas were generally low to begin with, but decreased even more with BRT in the first two sessions. Introduction of diaphragmatic breathing in session three resulted in tension increases in both areas, with smaller increases in session four. Measurement while seated upright, at the start of session five, produced relatively small frontalis increases and marked cervical increases. After Upright Relaxation Training, cervical tension showed large decreases, while frontalis tension increased somewhat. Tension levels in both areas were higher in the post-training assessment session than at the start of training.

Finger temperature during training is shown in Figure 5.9. On the first session, her temperature was at a moderate level, but on subsequent

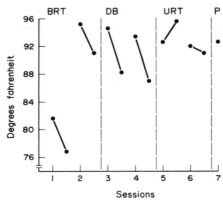

FIGURE 5.9. Finger temperature measures for Miss B. Phases and Legend are as designated in Fig. 5.5.

sessions temperatures started in the mid-90's, a ceiling precluding further increases. Temperatures were not maintained during training, and in most sessions they declined by about five degrees. Even diaphragmatic breathing training resulted in temperature decreases, in contrast to findings in some individuals by Bacon and Poppen (1985). During Upright Relaxation Training temperature seemed more stable. Her temperature remained high at post-training assessment. Overall, her temperature was related to BRS scores (Pearson r = −.67, p < .05).

Outcome. Weekly Headache Index scores are shown in Figure 5.10. During baseline, Miss B experienced at least one headache per week, which she said was common. She reported one major headache the second week of training, and one in the second week of the post-training period, but otherwise was headache-free. It should be noted that this was during the holiday period, which was a generally stressful time for her. Blanchard's formula for calculating outcome is as follows:

$$\frac{\begin{array}{c}\text{Mean Baseline}\\ \text{Headache Index}\end{array} - \begin{array}{c}\text{Mean Post-treatment}\\ \text{Headache Index}\end{array}}{\begin{array}{c}\text{Mean Baseline}\\ \text{Headache Index}\end{array}} \times 100$$

Values greater than 50% reduction are counted as a 'success'; values between 25% and 49% are considered to be 'slightly improved'; and those below 25% are considered treatment failures. According to this formula, Miss B experienced a 76% reduction in headache, clearly in the 'success' range.

Miss B did not like to take medication for her headache, and although she had prescriptions for ergot compounds she did not use them,

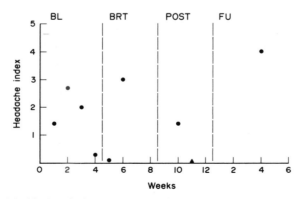

FIGURE 5.10. Weekly Headache Index scores for Miss B. BL = pre-treatment baseline; BRT = Behavioral Relaxation Training; POST = post-treatment period; FU = 6-month followup.

preferring over-the-counter analgesics. Her medication scores were as follows: Baseline = 4.75; Treatment = 0.0; Post-treatment = 1.0; Followup = 2.0.

During the six weeks of the six-month followup, she reported one severe headache which she said was the first she had had in the intervening period. Overall she reported a marked decrease in frequency; however, when one did occur, it seemed more intense. She noted this may have been due to her not being as 'used to' the pain.

At the followup interview, Miss B stated that she had ceased practicing the total BRT exercises after the end of training. But she reported that she was aware of her postures and breathing, and frequently engaged in 'mini-relaxation' during the day. She felt she was more aware of when she was becoming 'uptight' and could relax in those situations. She also reported that she had started jogging and she felt this also contributed to her remaining headache-free.

Discussion. The relationship between the various measures of relaxed behavior again points up the complexity of this response class. The close correspondence between the BRS and self-report suggest that Miss B was attending to the behaviors being trained, rather than other aspects of the situation as was the case with Mr. A. EMG levels also corresponded to BRS and self-report scores during initial training. Miss B's initial discomfort with diaphragmatic breathing was reflected in increased tension, as was the lack of bodily support while seated in an upright posture. Finger temperature, a measure of the visceral system supposedly related to the physiologic mechanism of migraine, showed a marked increase after the first training session. Although there was some temperature decrease during sessions, this measure was correlated with BRS scores.

Based on Blanchard's work with progressive relaxation training, we were prepared to supplement BRT with thermal biofeedback and stress management training. This was not necessary. One case does not herald a new cure for migraine. It is illustrative, however, of a technique which deserves further study, either by itself or in combination with other procedures.

The ease with which Miss B learned the relaxed behaviors, and her concomitant reports of calm feelings, provides a counterpoint to the difficulty experienced by Mr. A. Even so, things did not happen automatically for her. Diaphragmatic breathing was difficult for her to master, and it remained necessary for her to leave one hand on her abdomen to monitor her performance. But she practiced diligently, as evidenced by improvements within and between sessions, and achieved proficiency in skills which she could utilize in her daily activities. These two cases illustrate the extremes which a trainer may face. At this stage, it is not possible to specify the variables responsible for such differences. But it is obvious that with encouragement, persistence, practice, and adjustment of procedures for idiosyncratic needs, BRT can be employed for a wide variety of individuals.

TARGETS OF RELAXATION TRAINING

In his seminal book *Psychotherapy by Reciprocal Inhibition*, which sparked the current widespread interest in relaxation training, Joseph Wolpe (1958) proposed that the visceral responses resulting from progressive relaxation training were incompatible with, and 'reciprocally inhibited', the visceral responses characteristic of anxiety. The present book also proposes an incompatibility hypothesis, but across a wider expanse of behaviors. As presented in chapter 1, relaxation is viewed not as a unidimensional internal state, but as a response class across four modalities, which may differ among individuals and situations. Just as relaxation is a complex behavior, the behaviors which relaxation are intended to counter are also multidimensional. This book proposes that relaxed behaviors provide adaptive alternatives to complex emotional, stress, and pain behavior response classes.

A Taxonomy of Problematic Behavior

Table 5.1 presents a taxonomy of problematic behavior analogous to the earlier presentation of relaxation behaviors. Only an outline is provided, with frequently occurring behavior given as examples. For each response class, not all behaviors occur in all individuals in all situations, but there is enough consistency to give rise to a class name, such as 'phobia' or 'back pain'. BRT provides some alternatives to problematic behavior in each behavioral modality. Other relaxation methods, which emphasize a particular modality, may provide additional help for a particular disorder or individual client. This schema provides a basis for selecting among the various training methods—relaxation procedures which target behavior in a particular modality are expected to be especially effective in overcoming maladaptive behavior in that modality. Illustrations of this analysis are given for emotional, pain, and stress response classes.

Emotional Problem: Anxiety

Anxiety has been the dominant focus of behavior therapy since its inception, and has been the primary target of relaxation theories and therapies. Classification of anxiety problems is based on antecedent

Table 5.1. A Taxonomy of Problematic Behavior*

Problem behavior	Behavior modality			
	Motoric	Verbal	Visceral	Observational
Anxiety	Avoidance. Muscle tension.	Rules. Complaints. Anxiety Scale score.	Increased HR. Rapid shallow breathing.	Close eyes. Phobic imagery. Vigilance.
Anger	Aggression. Muscle tension. Restlessness.	Rules. Threats, curses. Hostility Scale score.	Increased HR. Increased BP. Rapid deep breathing. Sweating.	Stare. Selective listening.
Back pain	Guarding. Bracing. Muscle spasm. Inactivity.	Rules. Complaints. Requests for help. Pain Scale score.	Shallow breathing. Sighs.	Attend to pain. Seek distractions.
Cancer pain	Muscle tension. Inactivity.	Rules. Requests, complain. Pain Scale score.	Nausea. Cry. Irregular breathing.	Attend to pain.
Migraine	Muscle tension. Lie down.	Rules. Complaints. Headache Scale score.	Nausea. Cold hands, feet. Cry.	Close eyes. Cover ears. Pain location.
'Type-A' Behavior	Hurry. Activity. Muscle tension.	Rules about time, competition. Speech rate, prosody.	Angina. Increased HR. Increased BP.	Attend to time cues, performance standards.
Asthma	Avoid allergenic situations.	Rules. Complaints.	Wheeze, gasp.	Vigilance. Attend to breathing.

*Examples are given of emotional, pain and stress disorders for which relaxation training is often prescribed.

events which are believed to trigger the response class. Thus phobias are related to specific social and physical environmental events, agoraphobia to internal as well as external events, and 'free-floating' anxiety is defined by the absence of particular antecedents. A complete account of anxiety problems and their treatments is beyond the scope of this book. What follows is an analysis of anxiety according to the taxonomy given above, and a description of the action of BRT.

The goal of Behavioral Relaxation Training is to counter anxious behavior in the four modalities. Although training is usually carried out in a quiet environment, transferring skills to the 'real-life' environment is an important therapeutic goal. Methods of transfer range from 'train-and-hope', to simple exposure, to graded exposure with imaginal, pictorial, or *in vivo* cues. As with other relaxation training procedures, BRT is assumed to have prophylactic effects, in which regular practice in the home and work environment makes the trainee less susceptible to anxious arousal. An important factor governing this effect, as well as effectiveness in combating anxiety once aroused, is the ease with which the relaxed behaviors can be emitted in the natural environment.

Motoric Behavior. As shown in Table 5.1, this modality commonly includes avoidance of certain situations and events. When confronted with a fearsome situation, or even a few cues associated with such an event, motoric behavior such as increased muscle tension, 'freezing' or restlessness, and, if possible, escape, is likely. Thus a person who fears flying will avoid that mode of travel, and a person with public speaking anxiety will avoid professional commitments requiring such performance. Mr. A avoided travel requiring crossing bridges. When avoidance is not possible, increased muscle tension of the hands, arms, legs, and shoulders lead to 'white knuckles', trembling, or pacing. A person with 'free-floating' anxiety, not associated with any particular event, is likely to display general restlessness and aimless activity.

Relaxed motoric behavior is the primary emphasis of BRT. It is incompatible with actively avoiding or escaping a situation and it counters the tension and restlessness in which the anxious person ordinarily engages. Placing him or herself in relaxed postures is an overt action which a person can take when confronted with an aversive situation. This provides an experiential basis for a person to observe him or herself as calm and in control. Mr. A displayed relaxed motoric behavior while imagining the aversive scenes during desensitization.

Verbal Behavior. This mode of anxiety includes reports of environmental events and of the individual's reactions. In clinical or research settings, these statements are solicited on standardized lists and scales. Anxious verbal behavior may be formulated in terms of 'rules' (Poppen, in press) which exaggerate the aversiveness of the antecedent situation (e.g., spiders are especially huge and hairy, airplanes are incredibly noisy and unstable), emphasize the magnitude of the response (e.g., 'My heart is pounding so fast it will burst'; 'I can't breathe'), and magnify the consequences (e.g., 'I'm going to die!', 'I can't stand this!'). A frequent rule concerns the person's lack of control and inability to cope. Mr. A stated that he could not control his reactions when faced by a bridge and thus was incapable of driving. Such extreme verbal statements may add to the cycle of arousal, producing additional tension, visceral upset, and narrow observation. Verbal behavior is controlled not only by the events being described, but by audience variables such as attention and aid. Audience control is likely to be weak, in that anxious persons will address their comments to people to whom they would not ordinarily speak, such as the hapless stranger in the next airline seat.

Relaxed verbal behavior is generated by BRT's list of ten 'labels' of relaxed items, which the person can covertly recite. Self-statements on how to relax and be calm provides a reminder to the individual that he or she has a coping skill to employ in upsetting situations. Such statements are incompatible with anxious rules and may aid relaxation in other modalities as well. For example, verbal review of the relaxed behaviors can serve as cues to reduce tension and calm breathing, and can also focus observation on adaptive rather than maladaptive responding. It is unlikely that verbal relaxation alone is sufficient to counteract anxious rules, and additional interventions to replace this response category are needed. Mr. A's 'rules' showed a marked change after desensitization, and he confidently looked forward to the *in vivo* assessment.

Visceral Behavior. This domain of anxious behavior is characterized by heightened 'fight-or-flight' autonomic activity, though wide individual differences exist and objective measurement is difficult. Commonly noticed reactions include: rapid, pounding pulse, pallor, and 'cold feet' in the cardiovascular system; rapid, shallow breathing and dizziness in the respiratory system; sweaty palms, armpits, and upper lip in the sudomotor system; 'butterflies', nausea, dry mouth, and stomach rumbling in the digestive system. Mr. A reported the unusual response of a runny nose. In some cases, such activity is more severe prior to the actual event, as in 'stage fright' or 'performance anxiety'. Anxious visceral behavior may diminish as soon as the situation is over or it may persist for some time after. Some individuals respond viscerally to stimuli associated with the fearsome situation, such as a verbal description or a pictorial presentation, while others discriminate these events from the 'real thing' and react not at all. In cases of 'free-floating' anxiety or 'panic attack', there is no obvious relation between visceral behavior and particular events.

BRT teaches breathing control, directly counteracting the rapid shallow breathing which is part of some anxiety response classes. Other visceral systems may be influenced by slow, regular breathing and by decreases in muscle activity through relaxed postures. However, which systems are affected in what individuals under what circumstances remain a matter for further research. The absence or reduction of anxious visceral responding can serve as the basis for the observation and reporting of feelings of calmness and control. Mr. A experienced cardiac acceleration upon initial sighting of the bridge during *in vivo* assessment, but he did not observe this as aversive.

Observational Behavior. This anxious response mode is characterized by close attention to one's own visceral activity and muscle tension, and vigilance for external environment cues which might signal the onset of an aversive situation. In line with such narrow attention, the magnitude of fearsome events and reactions is exaggerated, verifying the anxious 'rules' described above. The person scans his or her environment for signs of impending doom and often misinterprets events in accordance with this view. Any creak or lurch of an aircraft is indicative of a crash; any insect is seen as a spider; any evaluation is seen as criticism. Similarly, one's own behavior is also magnified: one is 'drenched' with sweat; one's heart 'almost bursts' from pounding; one 'almost dies' from breathlessness. A person may close his or her eyes and ears to avoid or escape external stimulation, but covert events are more difficult to ignore.

As described above, relaxed postures and breathing provide a focus for relaxed observational behavior. This is both diversionary, distracting the person from attending to aversive external and internal events, and constructive, allowing the perception of control. Without the overwhelming nature of external threats and internal collapse, a person is better able to observe the relevant features of the environment for adaptive problem solving. During desensitization, Mr. A covertly observed the scenes on the hierarchy as well as his own calm behavior.

Conclusion. Relaxed behaviors provide effective alternatives for many members of the anxiety response class. But there are many other aspects of anxiety that are not addressed by relaxation training alone. A total behavioral treatment program requires a rationale for undergoing treatment, systematic exposure to fearsome situations, training in active, adaptive coping skills, a reformulation of 'rules', social reinforcement for improvements, and constructive support for setbacks.

Chronic Pain Problems

Thanks to the pioneering work of Wilbur Fordyce (1976), it is widely recognized that chronic pain is not a simple neurologic response to tissue damage, but is a complex class of behavior strongly influenced by social contingencies. Many aspects of pain behavior can be described by the taxonomy given above, and lend themselves to treatment by BRT.

Unlike problems which are episodic, chronic pain is always 'there', though it may wax and wane in intensity. This makes initial training difficult because it requires the trainee to immediately change some pain behaviors upon starting treatment, such as inactivity and attending to pain. On the other hand, this decreases the problem of transfer since the problem is less specific to particular environments.

Motoric Behavior. As illustrated in Table 5.1, chronic low back pain is characterized by many problems in the motoric domain. Guarding and bracing refer to stiff and awkward postures and movements to protect the back (Keefe & Block, 1982). Such action results in heightened muscle tension and asymmetric activity in many parts of the body in addition to the tension and asymmetry in the lower back. Inactivity refers to long periods of sitting or lying down. Generalized muscle tension and inactivity are characteristic of most types of pain, regardless of the site or physiological mechanism.

Inasmuch as BRT does not require muscular contraction, it is likely to be especially effective with conditions involving muscles that are already tense or in spasm. Similar considerations are important for joint problems, such as arthritis. BRT's emphasis on symmetry of postures is also beneficial for the twisted products of guarding and bracing, though difficult to achieve in early stages of training. A gradual approach is recommended. Supplementary training of particularly troublesome muscle groups with EMG biofeedback, as discussed later in this chapter, could provide a useful adjunct to BRT. It should be emphasized to the trainee that relaxation is a structured activity with therapeutic goals, and is not the same as lying on the sofa watching television.

Verbal Behavior. This modality includes reporting discomfort to others, primarily for purposes of attention and aid. Such aid has little lasting effect, and over a period of time the attention of friends, family, and medical staff extinguishes, resulting in escalating intensity and frequency of complaints and demands. Pain 'rules' are formulated, concerning antecedents (e.g., the incompetence of doctors, the greed of lawyers, the indifference of family), behavior (e.g., incapacity to function, the magnitude of pain), and consequences (e.g., nothing will change, insurance will run out). A pain sufferer often expresses angry statements at the failure of others to provide relief, and depressive statements of helplessness and hopelessness. Such rules may increase pain by creating an aversive social environment and focusing the sufferer's attention on his or her ailments and incapacities.

BRT provides some alternatives to verbal pain behavior. As in the case of anxiety, the list of relaxed 'labels' provides a prompt for trainees to engage in relaxed activities. This self-reminder of a coping skill can serve as an alternative to statements of helplessness. It can also direct observation toward adaptive rather than unadaptive behavior and sensations.

Visceral Behavior. This modality has not received much attention in chronic pain. Breathing irregularities, such as rapid shallow breathing and deep sighs, are common in low back and other pain conditions. Responses such as sweating, pallor, or nausea may occur in some people during a severe pain episode.

Visceral relaxation is targeted through breathing control, which counteracts hyperventilation. As described earlier, diaphragmatic breathing and decreased muscle tension may also have salutary effects on autonomic arousal.

Observational Behavior. As with anxiety, this modality is a major aspect of pain behavior. Close attention to pain and discomfort magnifies these sensations and can crowd out observation of any other events. Muscle tension, autonomic activity, and limitations of action serve as major foci of observation. A sufferer may seek to distract him or herself through passive observational behavior such as watching television.

BRT promotes a focus on self-control and adaptive behaviors of relaxed postures and breathing. Since bodily cues are often overwhelmingly aversive, it may be useful to supplement BRT with a procedure that diverts attention from this dimension. Guided imagery, which emphasizes other types of sensory cues, may be particularly helpful in this respect.

Conclusions. BRT can serve as a useful component in a chronic pain treatment program, but cannot be regarded as a panacea. Even within the domain of relaxation, it may be necessary to supplement BRT with additional procedures to overcome pain behavior in particular modalities. EMG biofeedback is recommended for treatment of specific muscle groups, and guided imagery for control of observational behavior. In addition, systematic contingency management programs are often needed to overcome inactivity and social dependency. Medication withdrawal, vocational and leisure skill training, and family education, are all important aspects of a comprehensive pain management program.

Stress Problem: Migraine Headache

Behavioral treatment of stress-related disorders has greatly increased over the past decade. Dualistic mind/body formulations are particularly prevalent (e.g., Stoyva, 1976). Stress responses are considered to be 'physiologic' and 'psychologic', analogous to 'somatic' and 'cognitive' anxiety. Physiologically, stress is regarded as an imbalance, primarily in the autonomic nervous system, but also involving hormonal, immune, and skeletal–muscular systems. Psychologic predispositions are considered to be important mediators of physiologic activity. Thus, according to this view, one's 'personality', 'response style', or 'mood', influences one's bodily reactions to the demands of everyday life.

Physiologic abnormalities define many stress disorders, such as asthma, coronary heart disease, or Raynaud's. In other disorders, notably headache and myofacial pain-dysfunction, the physiologic responses are not apparent and there is disagreement over what systems are involved.

Psychologically, scores on questionnaires concerning anxiety, depression, assertiveness, locus of control, affect, multi-phasic personality, hostility, and so forth are often found to be associated with various disorders. The most extensively researched relationship is that between 'Type A personality' and coronary heart disease (Booth-Kewley & Friedman, 1987). Though not as large, there is also a sizable literature on personality and headache (Blanchard & Andrasik, 1985). The magnitude of the relationships are small, but there is general consensus on an association between 'negative affect' scores, such as anxiety and depression, and stress disorders. The direction of 'causality' is not certain, and perhaps it is more fruitful to regard these relationships as interdependent. That is, anxious and depressive behaviors may well be members of the same response classes as stress disorders, all of which are in need of treatment.

Rather than the dualistic approach, stress disorders are considered to be response classes encompassing the four behavioral modalities as outlined in Table 5.1. Relaxation training, as well as other components of a treatment program, aim to modify behavior within and across these categories.

Migraine, like many stress disorders, is episodic, though it is assumed that there are characteristic inter-episodic behaviors that cumulate or otherwise predispose a person to an attack. Treatments are aimed at modifying these behaviors, thereby reducing the frequency of episodes; only secondarily is treatment concerned with what to do when an attack occurs. According to this view, regular practice of relaxed behaviors restores equilibrium to an imbalanced system, making the system less likely to cross some threshold into a maladaptive range. Once the throes of an attack have already begun, relaxation may promote restoring balance.

Motoric Behavior. Chronic elevated muscle tension in the head and neck is usually thought of as characteristic of muscle contraction headache, but there is evidence that levels are even higher in migraineurs (Blanchard & Andrasik, 1985; Olton & Noonberg, 1980). Some migraine patients display the busy, nonstop response style termed 'Type A'. Overt motoric behavior during a migraine episode is notably limited, as sufferers often cease all activity and lie down during a severe attack. Muscle tension, especially of the head and neck, may be markedly increased, resulting in additional pain.

BRT practiced on a regular basis, especially 'mini-relaxation' of the face and shoulders throughout the day, can reduce chronic tension. Longer practice periods can provide respite from a harried schedule, but need not be so long as to add to the time pressure. During the full-blown occurrence of a headache, relaxation can reduce the pain-induced tension cycle. Miss B found 'mini-relaxation' to be especially useful and practiced it regularly.

Verbal Behavior. Between headache episodes, verbal behavior may be characterized by the 'rules' typical of anxiety, depression, non-assertion, and so forth. Such a focus on environmental aversiveness and behavioral incapacity can interfere with effective problem solving and increase environmental stressors. During a headache episode, verbal behavior is more like that of chronic pain patients, with an emphasis on the intolerability of the situation.

As in the cases of anxiety and pain, the relaxed verbal behavior of BRT provides an alternative to the usual rules, plus the reminder that the person has a coping skill. The 'labels' can cue relaxed motoric, visceral, and observational behaviors during regular practice periods as well as during a headache episode. Miss B originally thought of her headache as the inevitable product of hormonal or other factors over which she had no control. She replaced this view with 'rules' concerning her own ability to control her reactions. Others might find that autogenic phrases contribute additional help in controlling visceral and observational behavior.

Visceral Behavior. Visceral activity plays a leading role in most formulations of migraine (Olton & Noonberg, 1980). Between episodes, migraineurs are supposedly characterized by vasomotor lability, with a tendency to respond to stressful events with peripheral and intracranial vasoconstriction. The person may observe these events as cold hands and feet, and as visual or other sensory prodromes. The headache itself is related to intracranial vasodilation, occurring as a 'rebound' to prolonged constriction. Gastrointestinal distress may precede or accompany the headache.

Reduced muscle tension and diaphragmatic breathing resulting from BRT may have a preventive or restorative effect on vasoconstriction during the non-headache periods. Miss B showed increased peripheral temperature after the first BRT session, and her temperature was correlated with BRS scores. Thermal biofeedback directly targets peripheral vascular activity, and may act synergistically with BRT in promoting vascular control.

Observational Behavior. During non-headache periods, migraineurs may be characterized by vigilance for events associated with headache, similar to anxious observational behavior. Some may be alert for foods causing vascular reactions. Others may be sensitized to events which are troublesome during a headache, such as bright lights or odors, or nausea related to menstruation. During a headache episode, sufferers try to decrease overt observation, darkening their room and insisting on quiet. Covert observation of pain and nausea may be particularly acute, similar to pain patients.

Relaxed observational behavior in migraineurs functions similarly to that described for anxiety and pain. During non-headache periods, it promotes the perception of control. Additional therapy procedures may be necessary to deal with 'superstitious' associations between environmental events and headache, and to promote functional observation of headache factors. During a headache, observation of relaxed postures and breathing may divert some of the focus on discomfort and promote a feeling of control. As with chronic pain, imagery procedures may enhance the redirection of observation.

Conclusion. BRT targets many migraine behaviors, but may not provide a complete program by itself, notwithstanding Miss B's success. Within the realm of relaxation, additional emphasis on verbal behavior, provided by autogenic training, on visceral behavior, provided by thermal biofeedback, and on observational behavior, provided by guided imagery, may be expected to facilitate treatment. In addition to relaxation procedures, a comprehensive migraine treatment program should include an analysis of possible dietary factors. For many individuals, training in social and interpersonal skills, such as assertiveness, communication, or time management, can make their environment less stressful. As with other disorders, rules emphasizing self-control and competence should be promoted.

Summary

Relaxation training is an integral part of the behavioral treatment of many disorders. The analysis presented in this chapter proposes that relaxation is effective not because it is an unobservable neurological state which reciprocally inhibits another, maladaptive, neurological state. Rather, the specific, observable relaxed behaviors provide adaptive alternatives to the numerous problematic behaviors which comprise a clinical entity. The various relaxation training methods emphasize particular response domains, which correspond in varying degrees to the problems characteristic of particular clinical categories, as well as to the idiosyncratic needs of individual clients. This analysis provides a rational basis for

developing treatment programs as well as generating many hypotheses
awaiting empirical verification.

COMBINING BRT WITH OTHER
RELAXATION PROCEDURES

As outlined in the first chapter, the various relaxation training methods
emphasize different behavioral domains and particular responses within
these domains. Although BRT encompasses all four modalities, it does
not cover all possible responses within each. In cases of particular
disorders, as described in the preceding section, or to meet the needs of
individual trainees, it could be helpful to broaden the scope of relaxed
behaviors by incorporating several methods.

A 'Shotgun' Approach

One strategy is to employ a shotgun approach, combining many
methods in the hope that some aspect will be appropriate for the idiosyncratic needs of each trainee. This approach has been advocated for a
variety of behavior change programs (Azrin, 1977). An example specific
to relaxation is the migraine headache program of Blanchard and
Andrasik (1985), which combines progressive relaxation training, autogenic phrases, thermal biofeedback, and guided imagery, thus targeting
motoric, verbal, visceral, and observational behavior modalities.

An advantage of a shotgun approach is that it increases the likelihood
of hitting a problematic behavior when the relevant variables are not
known. In a research setting, it offers the opportunity of reviewing a large
database after completion of treatment and relating client variables to
treatment and outcome variables. In this way a treatment program can be
refined to ultimately include only procedures pertinent to each individual. Refinement is important because the shotgun approach can result
in trainer and trainee wasting time on unnecessary, or—even worse—
counterproductive procedures.

Specific Combinations

In the best of worlds, a comprehensive behavior analysis of each client
would reveal the specific domains requiring treatment. Specific relaxation
methods which counteract particular problematic responses could then
be selected. Following is a discussion of the ways in which particular
combinations of BRT and other training methods could prove comp-
lementary.

Progressive Relaxation and BRT. Both methods emphasize the motoric
domain, but there are several ways in which they supplement each other.

First, when BRT is the primary training method, some individuals might have difficulty with a particular item. If this happens, a tense–release exercise of the relevant musculature aids in teaching control of that area. The control gained through tensing, and then releasing the added tension, may be seen as successive approximations toward sustaining a relaxed posture. For example, some people have difficulty with 'Eyes', continuing to move the eyes beneath closed eyelids. Verbal feedback may prove frustrating as the trainee is unable to directly control this action. Squeezing the eyes tightly closed has the effect of stabilizing the eyeball as well as directing observation to the proprioceptive sensations of tightness. Progressively releasing the tension allows the eyeball to remain stationary while maintaining the trainee's focus on the muscular sensations.

When progressive relaxation training is the primary method, BRT is helpful in showing trainees how their body should appear when the tension is released, and in aiding the release of tension in particular muscle groups. For example, in jaw exercises of the masseter and temporalis muscles, people release the 'clench' but often leave the jaw in a closed position. By training the relaxed open posture defined as 'Mouth', trainees are more likely to release more of the tension in the jaw muscles.

EMG Biofeedback and BRT. EMG biofeedback is another motoric procedure which can supplement BRT with a specific muscle group. For example, in learning diaphragmatic breathing, some trainees have difficulty in not using their trapezius. Their shoulders continue to rise and fall despite their best efforts to use only their diaphragm. EMG feedback from the trapezius provides the trainee with information of shoulder activity which is ordinarily imperceptible. Observation of this external signal can thus aid in learning breathing control.

The supplementary use of EMG biofeedback in treating chronic back pain has been mentioned. BRT teaches symmetry and generally reduced tension throughout the body. However, certain muscle groups may be hyperactive or spasmodic, and prohibit achieving relaxed postures in particular areas. For example, high and asymmetric tension levels in the spinea erectors could be troublesome, particularly in an upright seated position. EMG biofeedback focusing on those muscles would be synergistic to the overall goals of BRT.

When EMG biofeedback is the training method of choice, BRT can provide a 'platform' from which to begin training. As noted previously, EMG biofeedback may often serve as an indirect way to teach relaxed postures (Poppen *et al.*, in press; Schilling & Poppen, 1983). That is, trainees learn to reduce the feedback signal by reducing movements and shifting postures to relaxed ones. If still lower levels can be achieved than those reached by assuming relaxed postures, then initial BRT would be an efficient first phase, to be followed by biofeedback.

Thermal Biofeedback and BRT. Thermal biofeedback targets control of behavior in the visceral modality, namely vascular control, usually vasodilation. The controversy over the source of its efficacy—whether such control is achieved directly or indirectly through mediation in other behavior domains—has been described previously. A clinical goal may simply be to achieve warm hands, without regard to the mechanism, for example in the treatment of Raynaud's syndrome. In the long run, of course, it is important to be able to specify the controlling variables— which may differ across individuals. Until research untangles this knot, a shotgun approach may be useful. BRT reduces general muscle tension, which may contribute to vasodilation. Diaphragmatic breathing may also effect vasodilation. Training persons in these skills provides a means by which they might be able to achieve some success. Also, similar to the point made above with respect to EMG biofeedback, BRT can provide a base from which to measure additional vascular control.

Autogenic Training and BRT. Autogenic training targets verbal behavior, which in turn is assumed to control responding in the other domains. As with EMG and thermal biofeedback training, BRT could provide a foundation from which any additional effects of autogenic phrases may be assessed. From another point of view, BRT does not require much from the trainee in the way of verbal and observational behavior, and some individuals may 'let their minds wander' to events inconsistent with relaxation. Autogenic phrases provide verbal and observational behavior to supplement the labels and observation of postures provided by BRT.

Guided Imagery and BRT. Similar to autogenic training, this procedure's emphasis on verbal and observational behavior could provide a useful supplement to BRT in cases where attentional control is particularly difficult. As discussed in the case of chronic pain, the observational focus on constructed sensory events may provide an effective alternative to attending to pain. In combination with the motoric relaxation produced by BRT, this seems a potent package for countering many aspects of pain behavior.

DIRECTIONS FOR FUTURE RESEARCH

The basic empirical foundations for Behavioral Relaxation Training, and the use of the Behavioral Relaxation Scale, have been presented. But many assertions about relaxation in general, and about BRT and the BRS in particular, are hypotheses requiring verification. This final section brings together a number of research issues mentioned throughout the book.

These issues fall under two general headings, one dealing with the basic nature of relaxation, and the other encompassing its clinical significance. This is admittedly a somewhat fuzzy distinction, in that relaxation is always employed for clinical goals. However, some questions pertain to relaxation regardless of the particular clinical outcome, while others are more directly concerned with clinical results.

Basic Research Questions

The fundamental research issue remains; What is the nature of relaxation? Like Kipling's blind men and the elephant, various investigators have asserted that relaxation *is*, among other things, parasympathetic dominance, motoneuron quiescence, or a cognitive state of calm. Ignoring the problems of assessment for a moment, each of these may be part of the picture, but none is the whole 'elephant'. Perhaps a better metaphor would be the chameleon, reflecting the idea that relaxation is different things in different situations, for different people. As presented in this book, relaxation is a response class, across four behavior domains, which differs depending on environmental and individual variables. This point of view might be seen as enormously complicating the matter, greatly expanding the number of variables that must be considered. On the other hand, by changing the focus from a search for an elusive 'state' to a functional analysis of behavior, the chameleon can be better described.

Effects of Common Procedural Elements. One major question concerns what are often termed 'placebo' effects. These are more accurately called the effects of the 'common elements' of relaxation training procedures, as discussed in chapter 1. The distinction is that these are not inert procedures, as implied by the term placebo, but are active variables influencing behavior. Since they are an inextricable part of most training procedures, it is difficult to control for them by omission. That is, the appropriate research design is not a comparison of the presence vs. the absence of these variables, but a comparison of qualities and levels of these elements.

These variables involve certain antecedents, behaviors, and consequences. The antecedents include 'rules' — the rationale for training, an authority with special knowledge, an unwanted condition for which relaxation is said to be helpful, and a quiet place for training and practice. The behaviors include routine cessation from ongoing activities, observation of a repetitive low-intensity event, a comfortable posture, and self-report of progress. The consequences include social approval for success and support for failure, and possible alleviation of the unwanted condition.

The issue of interest is, what does BRT add to this general format? What are the effects of engaging in particular 'relaxed postures', and observing oneself doing so, as opposed to engaging in some other motoric and observational behavior? More generally, as outlined in Table 1.2, what are the effects of engaging in any of the behaviors recommended by particular training methods or theories of relaxation? Research comparing various relaxation methods addresses these questions. 'Placebo' comparisons involve rules and behaviors which, on theoretical grounds, are not believed to be 'active', but which still fit into the common element format.

Dependent Measures. The importance of assessing the behaviors being targeted by a particular relaxation procedure was emphasized in chapter 2. This is done routinely in BRT and biofeedback, where information on the target behaviors is an integral part of the training procedure. The BRS provides a measure for use with motoric procedures such as progressive relaxation and EMG biofeedback, as well as BRT. Measures of proficiency for the other procedures need to be developed.

In addition to assessing the specific behaviors targeted by a training procedure, it is necessary to measure behavior across several categories. Much has been made in this book of relaxation as a response class and the idea of multimodal assessment across the four domains of behavior. Most trainers assume that relaxation involves several responses within and across domains. These assumptions need to be made explicit through measuring the relevant behaviors. Furthermore, a procedure may not directly affect the targeted behavior. For example, thermal biofeedback and autogenic training, which target vascular responses, may achieve their effects through changes in motoric and respiratory behavior which are usually not measured. Multimodal assessment allows a greater chance of determining the controlling variables. A number of suggestions concerning multimodal measurement are given in chapter 2.

Clinical Significance Questions

Behavior During Training and Treatment Outcome. Related to the question concerning which responses are affected by training is the matter of how these are related to treatment outcome. This raises issues in the measurement of treatment outcome, such as validity of self and other report, use of concurrent vs. retrospective recording, physiologic assessment, length of followup, and so forth, which are beyond the scope of this book. The point here is that the relationship between how well people learn relaxation skills and treatment outcome is a testable assumption. All members of the relaxation response class need to be entered into the equation. An initial step in this direction is exemplified by Wittrock *et al.* (in press).

In cases in which there is a hypothesized mechanism of action in a particular behavior domain, such as muscle tension and head or back pain, it is particularly important to assess changes in that domain. This can lend support to the formulation, or suggest that another mechanism needs to be investigated. Measures need to be obtained not only in the clinic setting, but also in the trainee's home environment. Most treatment strategies assume that they are not simply providing a 'dose' of relaxation in the clinic, but that they are teaching a skill that generalizes or is practiced in the trainee's everyday environment. This is another testable assumption. Improvements in electronic technology and miniaturization makes portable EMG and visceral measures more available to clinical researchers, though these are still beyond the reach of practicing clinicians. The BRS and the Upright Relaxation Scale provide non-electronic measures.

For example, BRT, like progressive relaxation and EMG biofeedback, is assumed to target changes in motoric behavior (muscle tension) which is measureable by the BRS. Changes in BRS (and EMG levels) in the training and home environment can be related to changes in symptoms in order to test the treatment hypothesis. Observers can be trained in the client's home environment to score the BRS, as described in chapter 4.

Clinical Effects of BRT. Clinical outcome studies of BRT are needed. Many stress and pain disorders are assumed to have muscle tension or asymmetry as a major component. Tension headache, myofacial pain/dysfunction, and low-back pain, as well as general myofascial complaints, should lend themselves to treatment with BRT. Since BRT directly targets relaxed motoric behavior throughout the body, it has been suggested that it is more efficient than the other motoric methods, progressive relaxation and EMG biofeedback (Schilling & Poppen, 1983).

Chapter 4 called attention to the need for treatment of stress, pain, and anxiety disorders in special populations. It was proposed that the objective nature of BRT would make it especially efficient for such treatment (Raymer & Poppen, 1985). This proposal awaits verification.

As an aside, questions of treatment efficiency require a different sort of research design. The usual procedure is to employ a fixed number of treatment sessions with variable measures of outcome, such as average improvement or percentage of subjects reaching a criterion. Instead, it is possible to set an improvement criterion, both in terms of proficiency in relaxed behaviors and symptom change, and measure 'trials to criterion' as a dependent variable with the various relaxation procedures as the independent variable. This more closely approximates clinical practice, in which treatment continues until some level of satisfaction is reached (Poppen, 1983).

Another class of disorders for which BRT and diaphragmatic breathing should be effective are those which involve (or are assumed to involve) behavior in the visceral domain, specifically cardiovascular and respiratory response systems. These include asthma, panic attack, hypertension, and migraine. As with primarily motoric disorders, treatment comparison research is called for.

Disorders involving primarily observational behavior, such as neurogenic pain, are not expected to be strongly improved by BRT, which does not emphasize behavior in this domain. Observational methods like hypnosis or guided imagery should be particularly helpful. BRT may be combined easily with these procedures resulting in a more potent treatment than either alone. All the suggested combinations of BRT with other methods, as described in an earlier section, require empirical validation.

CONCLUSIONS

Early research and clinical application of BRET has been exciting to the author and his students. But conclusions concerning efficacy and efficiency are premature. It is hoped that this book will serve as an antecedent for many others to join in the investigation.

Beyond the specific issues of BRT and the BRS as means of training and assessing relaxation, it is hoped that the general conceptual framework presented will inspire a new look at this old topic. Presenting the various relaxation methods and theories from a single (behavioral) viewpoint allows a rational basis for comparison and testable conjecture. It is time to move beyond the 'pay your money and take your choice' stage to decisions based on rational and empirical evidence.

Appendix A

THE BRS SCORE SHEET

BRS Score Sheet

Client _____

Session No. _____ Date _____ Time _____

Breathing baseline ☐

− unrelaxed
+ relaxed

INTERVALS

	1	2	3	4	5	6	7	8	9	10	TOTAL
Breathing	− +	− +	− +	− +	− +	− +	− +	− +	− +	− +	
Quiet	− +	− +	− +	− +	− +	− +	− +	− +	− +	− +	
Body	− +	− +	− +	− +	− +	− +	− +	− +	− +	− +	
Head	− +	− +	− +	− +	− +	− +	− +	− +	− +	− +	
Eyes	− +	− +	− +	− +	− +	− +	− +	− +	− +	− +	
Mouth	− +	− +	− +	− +	− +	− +	− +	− +	− +	− +	
Throat	− +	− +	− +	− +	− +	− +	− +	− +	− +	− +	
Shoulders	− +	− +	− +	− +	− +	− +	− +	− +	− +	− +	
Hands	− +	− +	− +	− +	− +	− +	− +	− +	− +	− +	
Feet	− +	− +	− +	− +	− +	− +	− +	− +	− +	− +	

SCORE

EMG Level ☐   X̄ uV

Self-Rating: 1 2 3 4 5 6 7

123

Appendix B

WRITTEN CRITERION TESTS
FOR BRS OBSERVERS

Form A

1. List the 10 items scored on the Behavioral Relaxation Scale.
2. Which of the following are *not* considered to be relaxed behavior?
    - (a) chin sunk down on chest (*)
    - (b) shoulders sloped and even
    - (c) feet crossed at the ankles (*)
    - (d) eyes open and focused on the middle distance (*)
3. What is the optimal duration for a BRS observation period?
    - (a) 30 minutes
    - (b) 30 seconds
    - (c) 5 minutes (*)
    - (d) 5 seconds
4. If a trainee clears his/her throat during an observation period, this could be scored as unrelaxed
    - (a) Mouth
    - (b) Quiet (*)
    - (c) Breathing (*)
    - (d) Throat
5. How is Percent Unrelaxed calculated?

Form B

1. List the 10 items scored on the Behavioral Relaxation Scale.
2. Which of the following are scored as relaxed behavior?
    - (a) Eyelids closed and smooth (*)
    - (b) Lips closed with corners of mouth downturned
    - (c) Hands folded in the lap
    - (d) Heels together and toes apart

3. How long is breathing observed during each interval of the observation period?
   (a) 30 seconds (*)
   (b) 30 minutes
   (c) 5 seconds
   (d) 5 minutes
4. If a trainee scratches his/her nose during an observation period, this would be scored as unrelaxed
   (a) Face
   (b) Hands (*)
   (c) Head
   (d) Body
5. How is Percent Relaxed calculated?

Form C

1. List the 10 items scores on the Behavioral Relaxation Scale.
2. Relaxed breathing is defined as
   (a) The abdomen rises and falls while the shoulders remain stationary
   (b) No movement of the chest, shoulders, or body
   (c) Absence of interruptions such as coughing (*)
   (d) A rate lower than baseline (*)
3. Each interval in the observation period consists of
   (a) breathing observation—20 sec, observation of the other 9 items—20 sec, recording—20 sec
   (b) 60 sec observation for each item
   (c) breathing observation—30 sec, observation of the other 9 items—15 sec, recording—15 sec (*)
   (d) 60 sec of global observation for all items
4. If a trainee swallows during an observation period, this would be scored as unrelaxed
   (a) Mouth (*)
   (b) Throat (*)
   (c) Chest
   (d) Body
5. How is reliability between two observers calculated?

Appendix C

SELF-REPORT RATING SCALE FOR TENSION AND RELAXATION

1. Feeling More Deeply And Completely Relaxed Than I Ever Have.
2. Feeling Completely Relaxed Throughout My Entire Body.
3. Feeling More Relaxed Than Usual.
4. Feeling Relaxed As In My Normal Resting State.
5. Feeling Some Tension In Some Parts Of My Body.
6. Feeling Generally Tense Throughout My Body.
7. Feeling Extremely Tense And Upset Throughout My Body.

Appendix D

BRT HOME PRACTICE FORM

Name: _____

Date	Start	End	Self-rating	Difficult Items
_____	_____	_____	_____	_____
_____	_____	_____	_____	_____
_____	_____	_____	_____	_____
_____	_____	_____	_____	_____
_____	_____	_____	_____	_____
_____	_____	_____	_____	_____
_____	_____	_____	_____	_____
_____	_____	_____	_____	_____
_____	_____	_____	_____	_____
_____	_____	_____	_____	_____
_____	_____	_____	_____	_____
_____	_____	_____	_____	_____

Self-rating Scale

7 = Extremely tense throughout my body.
6 = Very tense in some areas of my body.
5 = Somewhat tense in some areas of my body.
4 = Neither tense nor relaxed. My usual resting state.
3 = Somewhat more relaxed than usual.
2 = Generally relaxed in most of my body.
1 = Deeply and completely relaxed throughout my body.

References

Agras, W. S., Taylor, C. B., & Kraemer, H. C. (1980). Relaxation training: 24-hour blood pressure reductions. *Archives of General Psychiatry, 37*, 859–863.

Arena, J. G., Blanchard, E. B., Andrasik, F., Cotch, P. A., & Myers, P. E. (1983). Reliability of psychophysiological assessment. *Behavior Research and Therapy, 21*, 447–460.

Azrin, N. H. (1977). A strategy for applied research: Learning based but outcome oriented. *American Psychologist, 32*, 140–149.

Bacon, M., & Poppen, R. (1985). A behavioral analysis of diaphragmatic breathing and its effects on peripheral temperature. *Journal of Behavior Therapy and Experimental Psychiatry, 16*, 15–21.

Barber, T. X., & Hahn, K. W. (1963). Hypnotic induction and 'relaxation': An experimental study. *Archives of General Psychiatry, 8*, 295–300.

Barkley, R. A. (1981). *Hyperactive children: A handbook for diagnosis and treatment.* New York: Guilford Press.

Benson, H. (1975). *The relaxation response.* New York: William Morrow.

Benson, H., Beary, J. F., & Carol, M. P. (1974). The relaxation response. *Psychiatry, 37*, 37–46.

Benson, H., & Friedman, R. (1985). A rebuttal to the conclusions of David S. Holmes' article 'Meditation and somatic arousal reduction.' *American Psychologist, 40*, 725–727.

Bernstein, D. A., & Borkovec, T. D. (1973). *Progressive relaxation training.* Champaign, IL: Research Press.

Blanchard, E. B. (1981). Behavioral assessment of psychophysiological disorders. In D. Barlow (Ed.), *Behavioral assessment of adult disorders.* New York: Guilford Press.

Blanchard, E. B., & Andrasik, F. (1985). *Management of chronic headaches.* New York: Pergamon Press.

Blanchard, E. B., McCoy, G. C., Musso, A., Gerardi, M. A., Pallmeyer, T. P., Gerardi, R. J., Cotch, P. A., Siracusa, K., & Andrasik, F. (1986). A controlled comparison of thermal biofeedback and relaxation training in the treatment of essential hypertension: I. Short-term and long-term outcome. *Behavior Therapy, 17*, 563–579.

Boice, R. Observational skills. *Psychological Bulletin, 93*, 3–29.

Booth-Kewley, S., & Friedman, H. S. (1987). Psychological predictors of heart disease: A quantitative review. *Psychological Bulletin, 101*, 343–362.

Budzynski, T. H., & Stoyva, J. M. (1969). An instrument for producing deep muscle relaxation by means of analog information feedback. *Journal of Applied Behavior Analysis, 2*, 231–237.

Cauthen, N. R., & Prymak, C. A. (1977). Meditation versus relaxation: An examination of the physiological effects of relaxation training and different levels of experience with transcendental meditation. *Journal of Consulting and Clinical Psychology, 45*, 496–497.

Cuvo, A. J. (1979). The multiple-baseline design in instructional research: Pitfalls of measurement and procedural advantages. *American Journal of Mental Deficiency, 84*, 219–228.

Davidson, R. J., & Schwartz, G. E. (1976). The psychobiology of relaxation and related states: A multi-process theory. In D. I. Mostofsky (Ed.), *Behavior control and modification of physiological activity*. Englewood Cliffs, NJ: Prentice-Hall.

Donney, V. K. (1986). *Teaching parents to conduct behavioral relaxation training with their hyperactive children*. Unpublished Master of Science research report, Southern Illinois University—Carbondale.

Fordyce, W. (1976). *Behavioral methods for chronic pain and illness*. St. Louis: Mosby.

Gellhorn, E., & Loofbourrow, G. N. (1963). *Emotions and emotional disorders: A neurophysiological study*. New York: Harper & Row.

Goldiamond, I. (1974). Toward a constructional approach to social problems. *Behaviorism, 2*, 1–84.

Goyette, C. H., Conners, C. K., & Ulrich, R. F. (1978). Normative data on revised Conners parent and teacher rating scales. *Journal of Abnormal Child Psychology, 6*, 221–236.

Hartmann, D. P., & Wood, D. D. (1984). Observational methods. In A. S. Bellack & M. Herson (Eds.), *International handbook of behavior modification*. New York: Pergamon Press.

Harvey, J. R. (1979). The potential of relaxation training for the mentally retarded. *Mental Retardation, 17*, 71–76.

Helfer, S. (1984). Systematic desensitization with behavioral relaxation training: Assessment of cognitive, physiological, and behavioral response systems. Unpublished Master of Science research report, Southern Illinois University—Carbondale.

Heller, T. (1982). The effects of involuntary residential relocation: A review. *American Journal of Community Psychology, 7*, 213–227.

Heide, F. J., & Borkovec, P. D. (1983). Relaxation-induced anxiety: Paradoxical anxiety enhancement due to relaxation training. *Journal of Consulting and Clinical Psychology, 51*, 171–182.

Heide, F. J., & Borkovec, P. D. (1984). Relaxation-induced anxiety: Mechanisms and theoretical implications. *Behavior Research and Therapy, 22*, 1–12.

Hersen, M., & Barlow, D. H. (1976). *Single-case experimental designs: Strategies for behavior change*. New York: Pergamon Press.

Hess, W. R. (1957). *Functional organization of the diencephalon*. New York: Grune & Stratton.

Hillenberg, J. B., & Collins, F. L., Jr. (1982). A procedural analysis and review of relaxation training research. *Behavior Research and Therapy, 20*, 251–260.

Holmes, D. S. (1984). Meditation and somatic arousal reduction. A review of the experimental evidence. *American Psychologist, 39*, 1–10.

Horner, R. D., & Baer, D. M. (1978). Multiple-probe technique: A variation of the multiple baseline. *Journal of Applied Behavior Analysis, 11*, 189–196.

Jacobson, E. (1929). *Progressive relaxation*. Chicago: University of Chicago Press.

Jacobson, E. (1934). *You must relax*. New York: McGraw-Hill.

Jacobson, E. (1938). *Progressive relaxation* (2nd ed.). Chicago: University of Chicago Press.

Javel, A. F., & Denholtz, M. S. (1975). Audible GSR feedback and systematic desensitization: A case report. *Behavior Therapy, 6*, 251–253.

Johnston, J. M., & Pennypacker, H. S. (1980). *Strategies and tactics of human behavioral research*. Hillsdale, NJ: Erlbaum Associates.

Keefe, F. J., & Block, A. R. (1982). Development of an observation method for assessing pain behavior in chronic low back pain patients. *Behavior Therapy, 13*, 363–375.

King, N. J., & Montgomery, R. B. (1980). Biofeedback-induced control of human peripheral temperature: A critical review of the literature. *Psychological Bulletin, 88*, 738–751.

Krmpotich, J. D. (1986). *Behavioral relaxation in an upright chair: An electromyographic analysis*. Unpublished Master of Science research report. Southern Illinois University—Carbondale.

Lacey, J. I., and Lacey, B. C. (1958). Verification and extension of the principle of autonomic response stereotypy. *American Journal of Psychology, 71,* 50–73.

Lang, P. J. (1968). Fear reduction and fear behavior: Problems in treating a construct. In J. M. Schlien (Ed.), *Research in psychotherapy,* Vol. 3. Washington, DC: American Psychological Association.

Lang, P. J. (1977). Imagery in therapy: An information processing analysis of fear. *Behavior Therapy, 8,* 862–886.

Lang, P. J. (1979). A bio-informational theory of emotional imagery. *Psychophysiology, 16,* 495–512.

Lehrer, P. M., Woolfolk, R. L., Rooney, A. J., McCann, B., & Carrington, P. (1983). Progressive relaxation and meditation: A study of psychophysiological and therapeutic differences between two techniques. *Behavior Research and Therapy, 21,* 651–662.

Lishman, W. A. (1973). The psychiatric sequelae of head injury: A review. *Psychological Medicine, 3,* 304–318.

Luiselli, J. K. (1980). Relaxation training with the developmentally disabled: A reappraisal. *Behavior Research with Severe Developmental Disabilities, 1,* 191–213.

Luiselli, J. K., Marholin, K., II, Steinman, D. L., & Steinman, W. (1979). Assessing the effects of relaxation training. *Behavior Therapy, 10,* 663–668.

Marks, I. M., & Mathews, A. M. (1979). Brief standard self rating for phobic patients. *Behavior Research and Therapy, 17,* 263–267.

Matson, J. L. (1985). Biosocial theory of psychopathology: A three by three factor model. *Applied Research in Mental Retardation, 6,* 199–227.

Mathews, A. M. (1971). Psychophysiological approaches to the investigation of desensitization and related procedures. *Psychological Bulletin, 76,* 73–91.

McGimpsey, B. A. (1982). *Behavioral relaxation training and assessment with developmentally disabled adults.* Unpublished Master of Science research report, Southern Illinois University—Carbondale.

Miller, N. E. (1978). Biofeedback and visceral learning. *Annual Review of Psychology, 29,* 373–404.

O'Leary, K. D. (1980). Pills or skills for hyperactive children. *Journal of Applied Behavior Analysis, 13,* 191–204.

Olton, D. S., & Noonberg, A. R. (1980). *Biofeedback: Clinical applications in behavioral medicine.* Englewood Cliffs, NJ: Prentice-Hall.

Ortega, D. F. (1978). Relaxation exercises with cerebral palsied adults showing spasticity. *Journal of Applied Behavior Analysis, 11,* 447–451.

Paul, G. L. (1969). Physiological effects of relaxation training and hypnotic suggestion. *Journal of Abnormal and Social Psychology, 74,* 425–437.

Peveler, R. C., & Johnston, D. W. (1986). Subjective and cognitive effects of relaxation. *Behavior Research and Therapy, 24,* 413–419.

Poppen, R. (1983). Clinical practice and biofeedback research: Are the data really necessary? *The Behavior Therapist, 6,* 145–148.

Poppen, R. (in press). Some clinical implications of rule-governed behavior. In S. C. Hayes (Ed.), *Rule-governed behavior: Cognitions, contingencies, and instructional control.* New York: Plenum.

Poppen, R., Hanson, H., & Ip, S. V. (in press). Generalization of EMG biofeedback training. *Biofeedback and Self-Regulation.*

Poppen, R., & Maurer, J. (1982). Electromyographic analysis of relaxed postures. *Biofeedback and Self-Regulation, 7,* 491–498.

Qualls, P. J., & Sheehan, P. W. (1981). Electromyographic biofeedback as a relaxation training technique: A critical appraisal and reassessment. *Psychological Bulletin, 90,* 21–42.

Reinking, R. H., & Hutchings, D. (1981). Follow-up to "Tension-headaches: What form of therapy is most effective?" *Biofeedback and Self-Regulation, 6,* 57–62.

Raymer, R. H., & Poppen, R. (1985). Behavioral relaxation training with hyperactive children. *Journal of Behavior Therapy and Experimental Psychiatry, 16*, 309–316.

Reinking, R. H., and Kohl, M. L. (1975). Effects of various forms of relaxation training on physiological and self-report measures of relaxation. *Journal of Consulting and Clinical Psychology, 43*, 595–600.

Reiss, S. (1982). Psychopathology and mental retardation: A survey of a developmental disabilities mental health program. *Mental Retardation, 20*, 128–132.

Reiss, S., Levitan, G. W., & Szyszko, J. (1982). Emotional disturbance and mental retardation: Diagnostic overshadowing. *American Journal of Mental Deficiency, 86*, 567–574.

Sargent, J. D., Green, E. E., & Walters, E. D. (1973). Preliminary report on the use of autogenic feedback training in the treatment of migraine and tension headaches. *Psychosomatic Medicine, 35*, 129–135.

Schilling, D. J., & Poppen, R. (1983). Behavioral relaxation training and assessment. *Journal of Behavior Therapy and Experimental Psychiatry, 14*, 99–107.

Schultz, J. H., & Luthe, W. (1969). *Autogenic training* (Vol. I). New York: Grune & Stratton.

Schwartz, G. E., Davidson, R. J., & Goleman, D. T. (1978). Patterning of cognitive and somatic processes in the self-regulation of anxiety: Effects of meditation versus exercise. *Psychosomatic Medicine, 40*, 321–328.

Schielkh, A. A. (1983). *Imagery: Current theory, research, and application.* Somerset, NJ: John Wiley & Sons.

Silver, B. V., & Blanchard, E. B. (1978). Biofeedback or relaxation training in the treatment of psychophysiologic disorders: Or, are the machines really necessary? *Journal of Behavioral Medicine, 1*, 217–239.

Skinner, B. F. (1953). *Science and human behavior.* New York: MacMillan.

Skinner, B. F. (1957). *Verbal behavior.* New York: Appleton-Century-Crofts.

Skinner, B. F. (1969). *Contingencies of reinforcement: A theoretical analysis.* New York: Appleton-Century-Crofts.

Skinner, B. F. (1974). *About behaviorism.* New York: Knopf.

Skinner, B. F. (1987). *Upon further reflection.* New York: A. A. Knopf.

Southam, M. A., Agras, W. S., Taylor, C. B., & Kraemer, H. C. (1982). Relaxation training: Blood pressure lowering during the working day. *Archives of General Psychiatry, 39*, 715–717.

Stoyva, J. (1976). Self-regulation and the stress-related disorders: A perspective on biofeedback. In D. I. Mopstofsky (Ed.), *Behavior control and modification of physiological activity.* Englewood Cliffs, NJ: Prentice-Hall.

Surwit, R. S., & Keefe, F. J. Frontalis EMG feedback training: An electronic panacea? *Behavior Therapy, 9*, 779–792.

Tarler-Benlolo, L. (1978). The role of relaxation in biofeedback training: A critical review of the literature. *Psychological Bulletin, 85*, 727–755.

Taub, E., & Emurian, C. S. (1976). Feedback-aided self-regulation of skin temperature with a single feedback locus. *Biofeedback and Self-Regulation, 1*, 147–168.

Taylor, S. L. (1983). *Behavioral relaxation training and assessment with traumatically brain-injured adults: Effects on motor performance.* Unpublished Master of Science research report, Southern Illinois University—Carbondale.

Wallace, R. K., Benson, H., & Wilson, A. F. (1971). A wakeful hypometabolic physiologic state. *American Journal of Physiology, 221*, 795–799.

Weitzenhoffer, A. M., & Hilgard, E. R. (1962). *Stanford hypnotic susceptibility scales.* Palo Alto, CA: Consulting Psychologists Press.

Werry, J., & Sprague, R. (1974). Methylphenidate in children: Effects of dosage. *Australian and New Zealand Journal of Psychiatry, 8*, 9–19.

Whalen, C., & Henker, B. (1976). Psychostimulants and children: A review and analysis. *Psychological Bulletin, 83*, 1113–1130.

Wittrock, D. A., Blanchard, E. B., & McCoy, G. C. (in press). Three studies on the relation of process to outcome in the treatment of essential hypertension. *Behavior Research and Therapy*.

Wolpe, J. (1958). *Psychotherapy by reciprocal inhibition*. Stanford, CA: Stanford University Press.

Wolpe, J. (1973). *The practice of behavior therapy* (2nd ed.). New York: Pergamon Press.

Wolpe, J., & Lang, P. J. (1964). A fear survey schedule for use in behavior therapy. *Behavior Research and Therapy, 2,* 27–31.

Wolpe, J., & Lazarus, A. A. (1966). *Behavior therapy techniques: A guide to the treatment of neuroses*. Oxford: Pergamon Press.

Zahara, D. (1983). *Behavioral relaxation training with traumatically head injured adults*. Unpublished Master of Science research report, Southern Illinois University — Carbondale.

Author Index

Agras, W. S., 26
Andrasik, F., 16, 23, 26, 42, 61, 99, 100, 113, 116
Arena, J. G., 26
Azrin, N. H., 116

Bacon, M., 16, 66, 67, 104
Baer, D. M., 78
Barber, T. X., 17
Barkley, R. A., 80, 86
Barlow, D. H., 75
Beary, J. F., 3
Benson, H., 3, 4, 5, 12, 16, 24
Bernstein, D. A., 15, 27, 28, 29, 41, 71
Blanchard, E. B., 16, 23, 24, 25, 26, 42, 61, 99, 100, 104, 113, 116
Block, A. R., 111
Boice, R., 39
Booth-Kewley, S., 113
Borkovec, T. D., 4, 6, 15, 27, 28, 29, 41, 62, 71
Budzynski, T. H., 15, 24

Carol, M. P., 3
Carrington, P., 4
Cauthen, N. R., 5
Collins, F. L., Jr., 3, 20, 27
Conners, C. K., 81, 82, 86, 90, 91
Cotch, P. A., 26, 42
Cuvo, A. J., 78

Davidson, R. J., 4, 5, 6, 7
Denholtz, M. S., 24
Donney, V. K., 86, 88, 89, 90

Emurian, C. S., 16

Fordyce, W., 23, 51, 110
Friedman, H. S., 113
Friedman, R., 5

Gellhorn, E., 2, 3
Gerardi, M. A., 42
Gerardi, R. J., 42
Goldiamond, I., 51
Goleman, D. T., 5
Goyette, C. H., 81, 86
Green, E. E., 15

Hahn, K. W., 17
Hanson, H., 15
Hartmann, D. P., 39, 41
Harvey, J. R., 70
Helfer, S., 93, 95, 96
Heller, T., 70
Heide, F. J., 4, 6, 62
Henker, B., 80
Hersen, M., 75
Hess, W. R., 3
Hilgard, E. R., 17
Hillenberg, J. B., 3, 20, 27
Holmes, D. S., 3, 5, 16
Horner, R. D., 78
Hutchings, D., 61

Ip, S. V., 15

Jacobson, E., 2, 4, 9, 13, 15, 28, 64
Javel, A. F., 24

133

Johnston, D. W., 5
Johnston, J. M., 39

Keefe, F. J., 46, 111
King, N. J., 16
Kohl, M. L., 23
Kraemer, H. C., 26
Krmpotich, J. D., 64

Lacey, B. C., 26
Lacey, J. I., 26
Lang, P. J., 7, 17, 93
Lazarus, A. A., 29, 94
Lehrer, P. M., 4, 5
Levitan, G. W., 70
Lishman, W. A., 77
Loofbourrow, G. N., 2, 3
Luiselli, J. K., 1, 20, 41, 70
Luthe, 16

Marholin, K., II, 1, 20
Marks, I. M., 93
Mathews, A. M., 23, 93
Matson, J. L., 70
Maurer, J., 24, 41, 43, 44
McCann, B., 4
McCoy, G. C., 42
McGimpsey, B. A., 74, 76, 77
Miller, N. E., 10, 16
Montgomery, R. B., 16
Musso, A., 42
Myers, P. E., 26

Noonberg, A. R., 15, 16, 25, 100, 113, 114

O'Leary, K. D., 80
Olton, D. S., 15, 16, 25, 100, 113, 114
Ortega, D. F., 70

Pallmeyer, T. P., 42
Paul, G. L., 17
Pennypacker, H. S., 39
Peveler, R. C., 5
Poppen, R., 7, 8, 15, 16, 22, 23, 24, 26, 27,
    38, 41, 42, 43, 44, 64, 66, 67, 80, 81, 83,
    84, 85, 104, 108, 117, 121

Prymak, C. A., 5

Qualls, P. J., 3, 15, 23, 25, 46

Raymer, R. H., 80, 81, 83, 84, 85, 89, 121
Reinking, R. H., 23, 61
Reiss, S., 70
Rooney, A. J., 4

Sargent, J. D., 15
Schielkh, A. A., 17
Schilling, D. J., 7, 8, 15, 22, 23, 29, 38, 41,
    42, 117, 121
Schultz, J. H., 16
Schwartz, G. E., 4, 5, 6, 7
Sheehan, P. W., 3, 15, 23, 25, 46
Silver, B. V., 16
Siracusa, K., 42
Skinner, B. F., ix, 9, 10, 15, 22
Southham, M. A., 26
Sprague, R., 80
Steinman, D. L., 1, 20
Steinman, W., 1, 20
Stoyva, J. M., 3, 15, 24, 112
Surwit, R. S., 46
Szyszko, J., 70

Tarler-Benlolo, L., 15
Taub, E., 16
Taylor, C. B., 26
Taylor, S. L., 77

Ulrich, R. F., 81

Wallace, R. K., 3
Walters, E. D., 15
Wilson, A. F., 3
Weitzenhoffer, A. M., 17
Werry, J., 80
Whalen, C., 80
Wittrock, D. A., 42, 45, 120
Wolpe, J., 2, 4, 15, 22, 28, 29, 51, 92, 93, 94,
    106
Wood, D. D., 39, 41
Woolfolk, R. L., 4

Zahara, D., 77, 79

Subject Index

Anxiety, 1, 3–7, 18, 23, 51, 62, 67, 77, 92–94, 99, 106–110, 121
Asthma, 3, 24, 66, 107, 122
Autogenic, 14, 16, 17, 20, 48, 99, 115, 116, 118, 120

Behavior categories
  covert, 9, 10, 13, 15–17, 24, 29, 59, 71
  motoric, 9, 10, 12–17, 29, 45, 46, 52, 59, 62, 94, 107, 108, 111, 113, 114, 116
  observational, 9–12, 14–17, 48, 59, 60, 62, 94, 107, 110, 112, 115, 116, 122
  overt, 7–10, 15, 29, 59, 71, 114
  verbal, 7–17, 47, 62, 94, 107–109, 111, 114, 116
  visceral, 2, 3, 5, 8–11, 14–17, 29, 47, 59, 62, 66, 94, 107, 109, 110, 112, 114–116, 121
Behavioral Relaxation Scale (BRS)
  definitions, 30–34
  observed period, 35, 38, 52
  reactivity, 35, 36
  reliability, 39, 40, 45, 75, 78, 81, 87
  relation to other measures, 42, 45, 76, 79, 82, 89, 94, 95, 97–99, 101–105
  scores, 42, 59, 76, 79, 82, 83, 87, 88, 94, 95, 101
  scoring procedure, 37–39
  training observers, 39–41, 87
  validity, 41–45
  video, 36, 37, 40
Behavioral Relaxation Training (BRT)
  acquisition, 52–57, 72, 78, 82, 94
  combination with other procedures, 68, 116–118

duration, 52, 75, 78, 81
feedback, 59–60, 63, 73, 95
practice, 52, 61, 65, 74, 75
proficiency, 52, 57–61, 73, 74, 78, 82, 87, 91
rationale, 51, 52, 72
setting, 50, 51, 61, 72, 74, 78, 81, 86
tokens, 73, 74, 81, 87
Behavioral taxonomy, 8, 9, 11, 13, 14
Biofeedback, 12, 16, 22, 24, 48, 71, 120, 121
  EMG, 14, 15, 20, 25, 26, 41, 45, 52, 70, 80, 112, 117
  thermal, 16, 92, 99, 105, 114, 116, 118
Brain-injured, 71, 77–80

Developmentally disabled, 70, 71, 74–77
Diaphragmatic breathing, 15, 61, 66–69, 101–105, 114, 121

Electromyogram (EMG), 2, 4, 7–9, 15, 24, 26, 43–46, 75–77, 79, 81, 82, 84, 86–89, 94–99, 101–103, 121

Guided imagery, 14, 17, 48, 112, 115, 118, 122

Headache
  migraine, 3, 47, 66, 67, 92, 99–105, 107, 112–115, 122
  tension, 24, 25, 46, 67, 121
Hyperactive children, 51, 71, 80–91
Hypertension, 23, 24, 47, 66, 67, 122
Hypnosis, 14, 17, 122

135

Imagery, 10, 11, 14, 16, 17, 67, 99
Instructional control, *see* Instructions
Instructions, 9, 10, 12, 13, 15–17, 23, 47, 53,
    58, 59, 66, 67, 70, 78, 97, 99

Medication, 80, 81, 86, 100, 104, 105, 112
Meditation, 3–5, 14, 16, 17, 62
Mini-relaxation, 61, 65, 107, 114
Multimodal assessment, 45–48, 120
Myofacial pain, 24, 46, 67, 113, 121

Pain, 1, 18, 23, 24, 46, 107, 110–112, 114,
    115, 118, 121
Panic, 23, 24, 47, 66, 67, 122
Phobia, 92–99, 108
Physiologic assessment, 2, 4, 23–26, 28, 100
Placebo, 5, 13, 20, 23, 41, 119, 120
'Problem of privacy', 22, 71
Progressive muscle relaxation, 2, 3, 5,
    13–15, 41, 42, 45, 48, 52, 62, 70, 71, 80,
    92, 93, 99, 105, 116, 117, 121

Questionnaire, 7, 81, 82, 84–86, 90, 92, 98,
    100, 113

Rationale for treatment, 6, 12, 17, 36, 66,
    67, 94, 110, 119
Rules, 12–14, 51, 99, 108–111, 114, 119, 120

Self-report, 5–8, 10, 13, 14, 16, 21–23, 28,
    29, 76, 80, 85, 94, 95, 97–99, 101, 102
Stress, 1, 2, 18, 25, 26, 51, 99, 112, 113, 121
Systematic desensitization, 2, 92, 93, 97

Temporomandibular joint (TMJ) disorder,
    see Myofacial pain
Tension/Relaxation Scale, 22, 48, 95, 101,
    102
Theories of relaxation and arousal
    autonomic, 2–4, 7, 11, 16, 24, 93, 106
    cognitive, 4–8
    dualistic, 4–7, 112, 113
    functional, 51
    somatic, 4–7, 24
    multimodal, 6–8, 45, 49, 100, 106, 113,
        119, 120

Upright Relaxation Scale (URS), 64, 65, 121
Upright Relaxation Training, 61, 63–65,
    101–103

About the Author

Roger Poppen received his undergraduate degree with honors in psychology from the University of Maryland—College Park, and his PhD in psychology from Stanford University in 1968. He joined the faculty of the Behavior Analysis and Therapy Program at Southern Illinois University in 1970 and is currently coordinator of that program. His research ranges from basic experimental analysis of animal and human behavior to applied clinical outcomes.

Psychology Practitioner Guidebooks

Editors
Arnold P. Goldstein, Syracuse University
Leonard Krasner, Stanford University & SUNY at Stony Brook
Sol. L. Garfield, Washington University in St. Louis

Elsie M. Pinkston & Nathan L. Linsk—CARE OF THE ELDERLY:
A Family Approach
Donald Meichenbaum—STRESS INOCULATION TRAINING
Sebastiano Santostefano—COGNITIVE CONTROL THERAPY WITH
CHILDREN AND ADOLESCENTS
Lillie Weiss, Melanie Katzman & Sharlene Wolchik—TREATING
BULIMIA: A Psychoeducational Approach
Edward B. Blanchard & Frank Andrasik—MANAGEMENT OF
CHRONIC HEADACHES: A Psychological Approach
Raymond G. Romanczyk—CLINICAL UTILIZATION OF
MICROCOMPUTER TECHNOLOGY
Philip H. Bornstein & Marcy T. Bornstein—MARITAL THERAPY:
A Behavioral-Communications Approach
Michael T. Nietzel & Ronald C. Dillehay—PSYCHOLOGICAL
CONSULTATION IN THE COURTROOM
Elizabeth B. Yost, Larry E. Beutler, M. Anne Corbishley & James R.
Allender—GROUP COGNITIVE THERAPY: A Treatment Method for
Depressed Older Adults
Lillie Weiss—DREAM ANALYSIS IN PSYCHOTHERAPY
Edward A. Kirby & Liam K. Grimley—UNDERSTANDING AND
TREATING ATTENTION DEFICIT DISORDER
Jon Eisenson—LANGUAGE AND SPEECH DISORDERS IN CHILDREN
Eva L. Feindler & Randolph B. Ecton—ADOLESCENT ANGER
CONTROL: Cognitive-Behavioral Techniques
Michael C. Roberts—PEDIATRIC PSYCHOLOGY: Psychological
Interventions and Strategies for Pediatric Problems
Daniel S. Kirschenbaum, William G. Johnson & Peter M. Stalonas, Jr. —
TREATING CHILDHOOD AND ADOLESCENT OBESITY
W. Stewart Agras—EATING DISORDERS: Management of Obesity,
Bulimia and Anorexia Nervosa
Ian H. Gotlib & Catherine A. Colby—TREATMENT OF DEPRESSION:
An Interpersonal Systems Approach

Walter B. Pryzwansky & Robert N. Wendt—PSYCHOLOGY AS A PROFESSION: Foundations of Practice

Cynthia D. Belar, William W. Deardorff & Karen E. Kelly—THE PRACTICE OF CLINICAL HEALTH PSYCHOLOGY

Paul Karoly & Mark P. Jensen—MULTIMETHOD ASSESSMENT OF CHRONIC PAIN

William L. Golden, E. Thomas Dowd & Fred Friedberg—HYPNOTHERAPY: A Modern Approach

Patricia Lacks—BEHAVIORAL TREATMENT FOR PERSISTENT INSOMNIA

Arnold P. Goldstein & Harold Keller—AGGRESSIVE BEHAVIOR: Assessment and Intervention

C. Eugene Walker, Barbara L. Bonner & Keith L. Kaufman—THE PHYSICALLY AND SEXUALLY ABUSED CHILD: Evaluation and Treatment

Robert E. Becker, Richard G. Heimberg & Alan S. Bellack—SOCIAL SKILLS TRAINING TREATMENT FOR DEPRESSION

Richard F. Dangel & Richard A. Polster—TEACHING CHILD MANAGEMENT SKILLS

Albert Ellis, John F. McInerney, Raymond DiGiuseppe & Raymond Yeager—RATIONAL-EMOTIVE THERAPY WITH ALCOHOLICS AND SUBSTANCE ABUSERS

Johnny L. Matson & Thomas H. Ollendick—ENHANCING CHILDREN'S SOCIAL SKILLS: Assessment and Training

Edward B. Blanchard, John E. Martin & Patricia M. Dubbert—NON-DRUG TREATMENTS FOR ESSENTIAL HYPERTENSION

Samuel M. Turner & Deborah C. Beidel—TREATING OBSESSIVE-COMPULSIVE DISORDER

Alice W. Pope, Susan M. McHale & W. Edward Craighead—SELF-ESTEEM ENHANCEMENT WITH CHILDREN AND ADOLESCENTS

Jean E. Rhodes & Leonard A. Jason—PREVENTING SUBSTANCE ABUSE AMONG CHILDREN AND ADOLESCENTS

Gerald D. Oster, Janice E. Caro, Daniel R. Eagen & Margaret A. Lillo—ASSESSING ADOLESCENTS

Robin C. Winkler, Dirck W. Brown, Margaret van Keppel & Amy Blanchard—CLINICAL PRACTICE IN ADOPTION

Roger Poppen—BEHAVIORAL RELAXATION TRAINING AND ASSESSMENT.